PUBLIC OPINION AND DEMOCRATIC ACCOUNTABILITY

PUBLIC OPINION AND DEMOCRATIC ACCOUNTABILITY

HOW CITIZENS LEARN ABOUT POLITICS

Vincent L. Hutchings

PRINCETON UNIVERSITY PRESS PRINCETON AND OXFORD

Copyright © 2003 by Princeton University Press
Published by Princeton University Press, 41 William Street,
Princeton, New Jersey 08540
In the United Kingdom: Princeton University Press, 3 Market Place,
Woodstock, Oxfordshire OX20 1SY
All Rights Reserved

Second printing, and first paperback printing, 2005
Paperback ISBN-13: 978-0-691-12379-0
Paperback ISBN-10: 0-691-12379-9

The Library of Congress has cataloged the cloth edition of this book as follows

Hutchings, Vincent L., 1965–
Public opinion and democratic accountability : how citizens learn about
politics / Vincent L. Hutchings.
p. cm.
Includes bibliographical references and index.
ISBN 0-691-11416-1
1. Political participation—United States—Public opinion. 2. Democracy—
United States—Public opinion. 3. Public opinion—United States. I. Title.
JK1764 .H883 2002
323'.042'0973—dc21   2002034647

British Library Cataloging-in-Publication Data is available

This book has been composed in Baskerville

Printed on acid-free paper. ∞

pup.princeton.edu

Printed in the United States of America

10 9 8 7 6 5 4 3 2

Contents

Figures

Tables

Preface

MY INTEREST in democratic accountability and its relationship to public opinion derives from two sources. First, John Zaller is principally responsible for introducing me to the vast literature on the importance of political information to the functioning of representative democracies. Second, Frank Gilliam's work first opened my eyes to literature demonstrating how the size of the black constituency influences political responsiveness. Throughout my graduate school career, and in my time at the University of Michigan, understanding these two ideas—the importance of political information and the ability of citizens to ensure accountability—has been my primary intellectual ambition. This book is the culmination of that ambition. Thus, before I thank anyone else for their contribution to this book, I thank my graduate school advisors, John Zaller and Frank Gilliam.

A considerable number of other people have also provided invaluable assistance to me on various stages of this project over the years. Perhaps chief among those individuals are the other members of my dissertation committee: John Petrocik, Kathy Bawn, and Larry Bobo. John provided a healthy and helpful dose of skepticism on the dissertation that would eventually evolve into this book. Kathy helped me to develop my ideas about representation. And last, but not least, I learned much of what a social scientist can and should be through my association and collaborations with Larry. I would like to think that I am a better scholar as a consequence of my interactions with each of these individuals.

The completion of this book would not have been possible without the intellectual contributions of a number of friends and colleagues who commented on all or part of the manuscript. First, Nick Valentino, my collaborator on a number of other projects, supplied very helpful comments on the first chapter. Moreover, Nick also co-authored chapter 6 and was largely responsible for collecting the content analysis data on gubernatorial candidates. Others who commented on drafts of this book include Ken Kollman, who provided detailed and prompt suggestions on the entire manuscript, Harwood McClerking, Taeku Lee, and Tasha Philpot. In each case, the book was clearly improved as a result of their input.

An earlier version of chapter 3 was published in the *Journal of Politics*. I thank Blackwell Publishing for permitting me to incorporate this article into the book. In addition, this chapter benefited greatly from the suggestions and helpful criticisms of Don Kinder, Nancy Burns, Hanes Walton, Brian McKenzie, Chris Achen, and Kathleen Knight. Finally, I thank

Lester Spence, Francis Rivera, Christine Garza, and Margaret Young for their coding of the content analysis data on the 1988–1992 Senate campaigns, which represent much of the contextual data in the book.

I am also indebted to the Center for Political Studies and the National Election Studies at the University of Michigan. All of the survey data in this book derive from this source. Clearly, this book could not exist without the voluminous data collected over the years by these institutions. Also, I thank Chuck Myers at Princeton University Press for his encouragement and enthusiastic support for this project.

Lastly, I wish to thank my parents, Charles and Thelma Hutchings, and my wife, Monique Ward. To my parents I owe my love of politics and my commitment to social justice. To my wife, I am indebted not only because she helped edit various drafts of this book but also because she provided the indispensable emotional and moral support necessary to complete a project of this magnitude.

PUBLIC OPINION AND DEMOCRATIC ACCOUNTABILITY

One

Issue Importance, Political Context, and Democratic Responsiveness

ARGUABLY the most important issue facing the country in 1968 was the war in Vietnam. By the beginning of that year, almost 30 percent of Americans had friends or relatives among the approximately half a million troops stationed in Southeast Asia (Lau, Brown, and Sears 1978). Additionally, the war was costing taxpayers well over twenty billion dollars each year, and roughly one hundred U.S. soldiers—and an untold number of Vietnamese—were being killed per week (Page and Brody 1972). Americans had become accustomed to, as well as disgusted with, the nightly images of the conflict that were displayed in their homes via the network news. Public opinion was sharply divided between supporters of the war and an increasingly vocal peace movement. This movement did not yet represent majority sentiment in the country, but the prospect that it might eventually influence American foreign policy seemed very real. Still, when the leader of the antiwar movement in Congress, Senator Eugene McCarthy, emerged to challenge President Lyndon Johnson for the leadership of the Democratic Party, many observers thought his chances for success were remote. Nevertheless, McCarthy engaged in a determined effort to unseat the president, beginning with an intensive campaign in the New Hampshire primary. McCarthy garnered a surprising 42 percent of the vote in this contest, compared to 48 percent for President Johnson. Although technically a victory for the president, many interpreted this election as a moral victory for the antiwar movement and a resounding defeat for the administration's policies in Vietnam. Shortly after the New Hampshire primary, Johnson withdrew from the Democratic primary. His presidency was effectively over.

On its face, the preceding account appears to be an excellent example of the significant role that voters play in our representative form of democracy. However, scholars of public opinion recognize that there is one important point missing from this story. Public opinion polls would later reveal that most of McCarthy's supporters in the New Hampshire primary actually favored an *escalation* of hostilities in the war rather than withdrawal (Converse 1975). Moreover, most of these voters mistakenly thought that McCarthy also favored a more "hawkish" stance. In short, one of the most glaring examples of the influence of public opinion in recent American history highlights the deficiencies of the electorate more so than its strengths.

Decades of public opinion research have provided voluminous support for this conclusion. For example, less than half of respondents in national surveys know both the name and party affiliation of their representative in Congress (Jacobson 1992). Further, barely a majority can provide this information for the senator seeking reelection in their home state. Typically, these percentages are even lower for congressional challengers. A skeptic might counter that this information is relatively unimportant as long as voters have a fairly accurate sense about where politicians stand on the issues. Unfortunately, even this information is unknown to much of the public. For example, over 40 percent of Americans either had no idea, or an inaccurate perception, of how their senators voted on the high-profile decision to go to war in the Persian Gulf or the confirmation of Clarence Thomas to the Supreme Court. When one considers that roughly half would accurately identify their senators' vote based purely on chance, this figure seems particularly low. Moreover, at least this many citizens are also unaware of the traditional differences between the Republican and Democratic parties on issues such as social welfare spending, social security, defense spending, and taxes (Bennett 1995).

All of this might suggest that politicians can safely ignore the opinions of their constituents. Strangely enough, this is not the case. An equally large literature indicates that politicians are often quite concerned with how their constituents will react to their policy positions. For instance, as explored in more detail in chapter 3, many senators publicly agonized over their vote on the Thomas confirmation because of concerns about constituent reaction. More than a few senators also declared that it was the toughest vote they ever had to cast.

The well-known political ignorance of the American voter juxtaposed with the genuine concern politicians express about faithfully representing their constituents begs the following question. Why do politicians worry about their voting record if voters are only dimly aware of this information? The aim of this book is to provide an answer to this question through an examination of survey data drawn from both Senate and gubernatorial elections. In brief, I argue that the perception of the American public as generally uninformed on political matters, although strictly accurate, is also misleading. In fact, under the right circumstances, voters are surprisingly well informed on the issues that they care about.

It is true that most citizens are often only vaguely aware of the issue positions of major political candidates (Bennett 1995; Smith 1989). This ignorance becomes more pronounced as one moves from presidential elections down to the less visible campaigns in Congress (Jacobson 1992; Mann and Wolfinger 1980; Stokes and Miller 1962). There are a number of reasons why this is so. Chief among these, ironically, is the generally high level of policy responsiveness. For example, presidential candidates, particularly the successful ones, generally agree with most voters on the issues (Page 1978). Additionally, members of Congress frequently share the same views and values as their constituents and thus need only follow their own preferences in order to successfully represent their state or district (Miller and Stokes 1963). In summary, voters often do not pay attention to politics because politicians see to it that they do not have to.

This is not to say that politicians never vote against their constituents' interests. I will argue, however, that this is not as common as many expect in large part because of the specter of constituent vigilance. This general tendency toward responsiveness makes it difficult for challengers to exploit an incumbent's record, and, consequently, voters are not regularly confronted with issue-laden campaigns. Only infrequently do incumbents fail to anticipate what some scholars refer to as the "potential preferences" of voters. I will show that when politicians do misread the public, however, interested voters learn about it, provided the media or political challengers convey this information to them. In short, voters are generally as informed about their incumbent's performance in office as they *ought* to be, given the relatively high levels of responsiveness, and they are about as informed as they *can* be, given the information made available.

This study provides a broad description and theoretical assessment of how voters observe and evaluate political actors. As indicated above, this book focuses entirely on state-level contests, but there is no reason why its conclusions cannot also be applied to national or local elections. The latter part of the book explores the factors that influence the prospective judgments that voters make about the likely actions of political candidates. The bulk of this study, however, focuses on the retrospective evaluations that voters make of their incumbent's actual performance in office. Specifically, I examine the process by which citizens acquire information about the performance of Senate incumbents and how they subsequently use that information to hold them accountable at election time. I refer to this process as "monitoring." The concept of voter monitoring is centrally important to my argument, but it cannot be examined independent of the context in which it occurs. It must be assessed in light of the political information that is readily available and the motivation of voters to pay attention to this information. As we shall see, previous works have not always considered each of these factors; consequently, they have underestimated the attentiveness and influence of the American voter.

To assess whether citizens are indeed capable of fulfilling their democratic obligations, I address four interrelated questions: (1) How much information on issues of public policy is made available by the mass media, incumbents, and political challengers? (2) How much of the information that is made available do voters actually receive? (3) Are citizens who are interested in particular issues also more informed about the candidate's position on those issues? (4) Do interested voters rely more heavily upon the information they receive when evaluating incumbents at election time?

In summary, the argument of this book is that the generally high levels of political responsiveness can be explained, in part, by incumbents' anticipation of constituents' likely reaction to public policy initiatives. This, and the ideology that legislators and constituents often share by default, generally lead them to come down on the "right," or at least the popular, side of an issue, thereby preventing challengers from exploiting their record. As indicated in the next section, other scholars have also noted the importance of the voter's latent political preferences (Arnold 1990; Key 1961; Miller and Stokes 1963). What has not been fully appreciated, however, is that the influence of latent public opinion hinges on how easily it can become activated. Indeed, if the voters' potential preferences cannot be easily activated—and if politicians come to recognize this— then incumbents will have little incentive to consider latent attitudes at all. I argue in this book that politicians are wise to consider the attitudes of their constituents, even when their constituents are effectively "asleep" or not actively engaged in policy debates. When incumbents do not correctly anticipate and respond to voter preferences, the mass media, interest group leaders, and potential challengers become alerted, thereby increasing the likelihood that interested voters will become informed. Moreover, once they are informed, interested voters will defend their interests and values at the ballot box.

This view of the mass public suggests that the electorate might best be described as a loose collection of "sleeping giants." These giants are not routinely vigilant, and in any case they do not all share the same political priorities. When the interests or values of one or more of these giants are at stake in a political contest, however, they can become surprisingly alert. Of course, this attentiveness is contingent on the presence of favorable contextual conditions, such as the availability of sufficient political information. When political elites provide this information, interested members of the public pay attention. Conversely, when elites neglect their responsibility, the sleeping giants continue their slumber.

Theories of the Link between Public Opinion and Public Policy

When the framers of the Constitution designed our system of government, they envisioned the legislative branch, especially the House of Representatives, as the most important and the most responsive to the people (Hamilton, Madison, and Jay 1961). Indeed, contrary to popular perceptions, there is now ample evidence showing that the voting behavior of members of Congress adhere closely to the preferences of their constituents (Bartels 1991; Jackson and King 1989; Jacobson 1992; Kingdon 1989; Miller and Stokes 1963; Overby et al. 1992; Powell 1982; Shapiro et al. 1990; Whitby and Gilliam 1991). While at first glance this evidence suggests the existence of a vigilant and attentive citizenry, decades of research in public opinion offer little support for this view. Researchers in this field have consistently shown that the electorate is generally uninformed and uninterested in issues of public policy (Campbell et al. 1960; Conover and Feldman 1981; Converse 1964, 1975, 1990; Smith 1989). Moreover, some scholars go a step further, arguing that, in spite of steady increases in education, levels of political information are not likely to increase substantially in the foreseeable future (Bennett 1995; Knight 1990; Nie, Junn, and Stehlik-Barry 1996; Smith 1989).

In short, previous research shows that legislators are generally responsive, but that this is not due to active monitoring by the public. This conclusion is puzzling. The framers of the Constitution expected the electorate to assess the performance of their representatives and periodically remove nonresponsive legislators from office. Thus, a vigilant citizenry was regarded as one of the chief mechanisms for ensuring democratic accountability (Dahl 1989; Hamilton, Madison, and Jay 1961). But if the electorate is indeed uninformed, they may be ill prepared to review the performance of their representatives, as the framers anticipated. What reasons, then, are there for lawmakers, or any other group of elected officials, to be responsive? More importantly, what penalties (if any) can legislators realistically expect to suffer if they do not faithfully represent their constituents?

Resolving this apparent contradiction is of more than academic importance. If voters are politically inattentive, then elected officials can ignore constituent opinion with impunity. Other scholars have also recognized this paradox and have developed several models that may account for this prima facie inconsistency (Erikson and Luttbeg 1973; Fiorina 1974; Jacobson and Kernell 1981; Miller and Stokes 1963). These models, although not mutually exclusive, invoke one of four main explanations: the general partisan or ideological orientation of the district; the ability of the electorate as a whole to cancel out the weaknesses of individual voters; the mediating role of organized interest groups; and elite attentiveness to, or anticipation of, constituency preferences.

District Political Orientation

According to the first explanation, policy agreement between constituents and legislators occurs primarily because of the manner in which many political jurisdictions are drawn. Specifically, most congressional districts are typically quite homogenous, both politically and socially. Even when there is significant ideological heterogeneity, many states and districts tend to have a dominant political orientation. Thus, the kind of representative most likely to be elected from such districts will tend to share this orientation. As a result, all that these legislators need do is to follow the dictates of their own conscience in order to represent their constituents effectively as well. This seems especially plausible in more homogeneous states or districts (Erikson 1978; Fiorina, 1974; Key 1961; Miller and Stokes 1963; Powell 1982).

In an elaboration on this model, representation may come about indirectly through voter reliance on party identification. According to this explanation, many political jurisdictions have a dominant partisan character just as they have a dominant ideological character. Because voting decisions rely heavily on partisan identification, members of the dominant party are far more likely to attain political office. Consequently, because partisan identification generally corresponds closely with issue preferences among both the elite and the mass public, legislators typically end up representing their districts even though voters do not consciously consider issues at election time (Erikson 1978; Franklin 1984; Pomper 1972; Popkin 1991; Repass 1971; Stokes and Miller 1962).

Preference Aggregation

A second manner through which the deficiencies of the electorate can be reconciled with widespread evidence of congressional responsiveness is preference aggregation. This view does not dispute the fact that most citizens are uninterested in politics and uninformed about policy debates at the elite level. However, proponents of this argument maintain that *collective* public opinion is often remarkably informed and influential (Abramowitz 1988; Condorcet 1785; Converse 1990; Page and Shapiro 1992).

Page and Shapiro (1992) offer perhaps the most detailed exposition of this account. They argue that, contrary to the view of many experts, collective public opinion is frequently stable (although not fixed), is coherently organized, takes into account the best available information, and changes in predictable and reasonable ways. In short, collective public opinion is rational. This can occur because most citizens are not terribly interested in politics and are not often critical of the political views they are exposed to and subsequently accept. This tendency to internalize politically inconsistent messages can result in seemingly random fluctuations in individual policy preferences. However, Page and Shapiro argue that the high levels of variance apparent in individual issue positions often mask a "true" underlying attitude.[1] When examined at the aggregate level, these fluctuations cancel out to reveal a public opinion responsive to elite behavior and one in which policy questions have a nontrivial impact on election outcomes (Erikson and Wright 1989; Kahn and Kenny 1999; Wright and Berkman 1986). According to Erikson and Wright, the "electorate is much more capable in the aggregate than as individual voters. It is as though all our individual ignorance and misinformed judgments cancel out, so that average perceptions and judgments are responsive to what candidates say and do. The result is perhaps a more representative Congress than the electorate sometimes seems to deserve" (114).

Interest Group Pressure

A third explanation for policy responsiveness relies less on the abilities of the average citizen and more on the presence of organized pressure groups (Blumer 1948; Erikson and Lutbegg 1973; Truman 1971). These groups can often effectively influence Congress because of their ability to identify and mobilize the inchoate interests of like-minded citizens through television advertising campaigns, petitions drives, and organized rallies (Kollman 1998). More recently, interest groups have also begun to rely on Internet-based techniques, or "cyber-lobbying," to organize potential followers and bring pressure to bear on Congress (Davidson and Oleszek 1998). This strategy of "outside lobbying" is often accompanied by more traditional efforts to influence legislation, such as providing policy information and technical expertise, or campaign contributions (Davidson and Oleszek 1998; Hall and Wayman 1990; Kingdon 1989). Thus, to the extent that interest groups are representative of constituent opinion, ordinary citizens may still exert an influence on their political representatives in spite of their inattentiveness. This is because it is interest groups that are actively monitoring politicians and not the average voter.

Potential Preferences

Finally, as indicated above, some scholars maintain that even in the face of voter ignorance, politicians have an incentive to be responsive because of their perceptions of the latent or potential preferences of inattentive citizens (Arnold 1990; Erikson and Lutbeg 1973; Fenno 1978; Fiorina 1974; Key 1961; Kingdon 1989; Miller and Stokes 1963). This explanation will be referred to as the potential preferences model. According to this model, legislators will tend to be responsive as long as they are convinced that someone (particularly a would-be challenger) is paying attention and might inform their constituents at election time.

Miller and Stokes explain the influence of the voter's potential preferences on legislative behavior in their 1963 article, "Constituency Influence in Congress."

> By voting correctly on [the issues, House members] are unlikely to increase their visibility to constituents. Nevertheless, the fact of constituency influence, backed by potential sanctions at the polls, is real enough. That these potential sanctions are all too real is best illustrated in the election of 1958 by the reprisal against Representative Brooks Hays in Arkansas' Fifth District. Although the perception of Hays as too moderate on civil rights resulted more from his service as intermediary between the White House and Governor Faubus in the Little Rock school crisis than from his record in the House, the victory of Dale Alford as a *write-in candidate* was a striking reminder of what can happen to a Congressman who gives his foes a powerful issue to use against him. (55; italics added)

Generally speaking, then, the models outlined above view the mechanism of representation as deriving either from lack of serious divisions within the political jurisdiction resulting in a shared ideological orientation between legislator (or political representative more generally) and constituent, the effects of aggregation, the influence of interest groups, or the potential attentiveness of the electorate. Although each of the models offers a persuasive explanation for legislative responsiveness, none of them is entirely satisfactory. Moreover, they generally provide only a limited role for the electorate. For example, the first model neither expects nor requires any direct monitoring on the part of most voters. At most, this model allows voters to exercise their influence on policy through their selection of partisan representatives. Beyond that, the average voter should demonstrate little active engagement in the political process.

Clearly, partisanship is an important component in ensuring legislative accountability, but relying solely on a candidate's party as an indication of their issue positions can also be misleading. Although there is considerable variance between the two major parties on numerous issues, there are also many issues on which there is considerable variance *within* the parties. For example, Democrats tend to be the more liberal party on the abortion question, yet in Louisiana all four Democratic House members along with the two Democratic senators scored a perfect 0 on the National Abortion Rights Action League (NARAL) index in 1990.[2] There were also few partisan differences among House members on abortion this year in states such as Connecticut, Idaho, Kentucky, Maine, Mississippi, Washington, and elsewhere in the country.

Differences on important policy questions within the major parties are at times even greater in the Senate. In 1990 alone, senators of the same party representing the same state differed by at least 30 points on the NARAL index in Alabama, Alaska, Illinois, Kansas, Missouri, Nebraska, Nevada, New Hampshire, North Dakota, Oregon, and Washington. Moreover, Republican senators scored uncharacteristically high (i.e., 60 or above) on this measure in seven states in 1990. In the same year, six of the seventeen Democratic senators facing reelection also received scores of 60 or higher on the conservative National Security Index of congressional votes (NSI). Clearly, knowing which party a politician belongs to reveals a great deal about his or her issue positions, but it does not reveal everything. Therefore, it seems likely that the generally high levels of congressional responsiveness do not occur simply because of the partisan or ideological orientation of the district.

Preference aggregation models find that an informed consideration of the issues does influence the collective voting decisions of the electorate. Other scholars, however, have found that the aggregation process does not quite live up to its billing. Althaus (1998), for example, reports that the collective opinion represented in surveys often misrepresents the distribution of attitudes in society. In short, aggregate support for or opposition to some policies would look considerably different if the average voter were more informed about politics (also see Bartels 1996). Converse (1990) also points out that preference aggregation models often overlook the fact that some citizens are vastly more informed than are others. He concludes that the "rationality" attributed to aggregate public opinion derives disproportionately from the relative few who are especially well informed.

There is some controversy in the literature as to the identity of this informed group of voters. Some argue that there is a small group of citizens who are typically attentive to a broad range of issues whereas most voters have little or no interest in politics (Price and Zaller 1993; Zaller 1992). If this is so, then the influence of aggregate public opinion can more accurately be described as the influence of the relatively few Americans who are unusually attentive to politics. According to another view, one adopted in this book and explored more fully in the next section, the more informed sentiment at the core of aggregate public opinion differs from issue to issue. Converse (1964) referred to these groups as "issue publics." Subsequent chapters will demonstrate that aggregate public opinion is indeed attentive to the activities of incumbents. However, issue publics are as likely as citizens more generally informed about politics to represent the driving force behind this attentiveness.

Pressure group models also expect little active monitoring by most citizens. Instead, interest group leaders watch over public officials in order to safeguard the welfare of their members. There is at least one reason why this explanation cannot fully account for the relationship between public opinion and public policy. Sometimes group leaders and rank-and-file members disagree on major policy questions. A conspicuous example is provided in chapter 3's discussion of the Clarence Thomas confirmation battle. Mainstream black political leaders opposed this unusually controversial nomination, but opinion polls showed that most African Americans supported Thomas. In the end, many Democratic senators also sided with Thomas. Presumably, these senators were more concerned with the opinion of their black constituents than that of African American group leaders. This concern could only be justified if the average black voter, and not merely black opinion leaders, were more informed about this vote than other Americans.

Even if one assumes that, on the majority of issues, interest group leaders do most of the heavy lifting in a representative democracy, there is still an important role for ordinary citizens. If the threats of an interest group regarding voter mobilization are to have any credibility among politicians, then group leaders must demonstrate an ability to alert and mobilize its membership. In other words, the "sleeping giant" must stir, at least occasionally, if governmental leaders are to pay it any heed.

Unlike district orientation models, potential preference models do not explicitly preclude issue-based monitoring, but they do suggest that legislators try to anticipate potential voter concerns and defuse them before they arise. Hence, as with the pressure group models, actual voter attentiveness is unnecessary and unusual. Still, representatives rarely have complete information about their constituents' current or future preferences, and so they may still unwittingly provoke voters and thereby encourage would-be challengers. Moreover, the heterogeneity of their state or district may also preclude a cost-free vote on some issues (Hutchings, McClerking, and Charles 2000). Of course this is only problematic if the electorate is informed or can easily become so. If the likelihood of voters becoming informed is indeed low, then legislators will typically suffer no costs for incorrectly anticipating voter preferences.

None of the general models described above fully explains the observed correlation between legislators' roll call votes and district/state opinion. Shared partisanship and ideology undoubtedly play an important role, but there is sufficient variation within and across congressional parties to undermine confidence in this explanation. The aggregation model seems to require at least some voters to have informed opinions, but it does not specify which voters are informed and under what circumstances they become so. Finally, the pressure group and potential preferences models suggest a more indirect role for voters in ensuring congressional responsiveness. Still, both would have little influence over policy makers unless there are at least occasional instances when voters demonstrate significant interest in, and knowledge about, matters of public policy.

None of these broader explanations is the only way to account for the relationship between constituent attitudes and legislative outcomes. Some scholars simply reject the premise that substantial levels of political knowledge are required in order for the mass public to effectively monitor their elected representatives. Some of these researchers argue that many citizens rely on information "short cuts," or heuristics, to direct their political judgments (Grofman and Norrander 1990; Lupia 1994; Lupia and McCubbins 1998; Popkin 1991). Others argue that voter impressions of political candidates and parties are constantly updated with new information even though much of that information is quickly forgotten (Fiorina 1981; Lodge, McGraw, and Stroh 1989; Lodge, Steenbergen, and Brau 1995). I am generally persuaded by both sets of explanations. However, they do not negate the basic importance of voter monitoring. If politicians behave in a manner inconsistent with the preferences of their constituents, then the only way for voters to hold them accountable is if they learn about this action and vote accordingly at election time. Whether this information is gained via shortcuts or more traditional routes ultimately involves the *process* of attentiveness and not the *product*. This book is more concerned with whether citizens gain the necessary political information than with precisely how they gain it. Further, whether or not this information influences political impressions but is quickly forgotten should not affect whether the voting record of members of Congress influence citizens' vote choice. Under either scenario, voters must reward their "friends" and punish their "enemies" at the ballot box in order for them to play any direct role in ensuring legislative responsiveness.

An Alternative Framework for Understanding the Relationship between Public Opinion and Policy Responsiveness

This study argues that voter monitoring does not play merely a passive, or indirect, role in helping to guarantee legislative responsiveness. Along with the other theories discussed above, voter monitoring (or at least the specter of it) plays a critical role in the relationship between constituent attitudes and political representation. To understand this relationship, we must turn our attention to two interrelated sets of concepts: individual motivation and contextual factors that promote heightened political attentiveness.

The motivation to learn about politics is central to the thesis of this book. A growing body of literature suggests that this motivation can sometimes compensate for traditional deficiencies in political information. More specifically, many scholars argue that shifting groups of citizens are remarkably informed about, and more likely to vote on the basis of, issues that they perceive as important (Campbell 2003; Hutchings 2001; Iyengar 1990; Krosnick 1988, 1990b; Krosnick, Berent, and Boninger 1994; McGraw and Pinney 1990; Popkin 1991). Previous research indicates that these perceptions generally originate from at least one of three sources: self-interest, group interests, or core values (Boninger, Krosnick, and Berent 1995; Campbell, et al. 1960; Conover 1984, 1985; Popkin 1991).[3] This helps to explain why Iyengar (1990) found that Jewish Americans were more informed than other citizens about Middle East politics, blacks were more informed than whites about civil rights issues, and blue-collar workers were more informed than non–group members about the economy.[4] Philip Converse, in "The Nature of Belief Systems in Mass Publics"(1964), was among the first to recognize the importance of individual motivation (see also Key, 1961; Truman 1971). He noted that

> different controversies excite different people to the point of real opinion formation. One man takes an interest in policies bearing on the Negro and is relatively indifferent to or ignorant about controversies in other areas. His neighbor may have few crystallized opinions on the race issue, but he may find the subject of foreign aid very important. Such *sharp divisions of interest* are part of what the term "issue public" is intended to convey. (245; italics added)

There is an additional reason to believe that voters tend to focus on a few, mostly group-relevant issues. The costs of becoming well informed on more than a few issues are too great for most people (Downs 1957; Fiske and Taylor 1991; Lau and Sears 1986). Concentrating on a relatively narrow range of issues is one way of minimizing these costs. Citizens also rely on partisan cues, friends and co-workers, or formal groups such as unions and churches as sources of political information (Dawson 1994; Huckfeldt 1986; Tate 1993). Previous studies on the role of issues in congressional elections have often overlooked or understated the importance of issue salience (Abramowitz 1988; Erikson and Wright 1989; Mann and Wolfinger 1980; Stokes and Miller 1962; Wright and Berkman 1986).[5] Consequently, they have understated the influence that policy concerns play in voters' political judgments and the role that constituent preferences play in affecting political outcomes.

Yet another reason for believing that the electorate is primarily made up of citizens who are most attentive to issues they view as important is that legislators themselves view the public in this way (Fiorina 1974). For example, Fenno (1978) reports a House member stating that

> '[t]here isn't one voter in 20,000 who knows my voting record ... except on that one thing that affects him.' And another said, 'Only a few discerning people know my voting record: *labor, the environmentalists, and the Chamber of Commerce.*' But it is, of course, the voter dissatisfied with 'that one thing that affects him' or the 'few discerning people' who will press for explanations. (142; italics added)

Kingdon (1989) reaches similar conclusions. He notes that many representatives feel that while their constituencies were generally ignorant of their votes in Washington, subgroups within the district could be extremely aware, depending on the issue. One member of Congress interviewed by Kingdon was particularly concerned about the attentiveness of African Americans and organized labor.

> [M]ost of my constituents don't care [about the Adam Clayton Powell vote]. . . . But there is one group that will notice—the black community. They'll take account of what you do, and hold it against you if you go wrong. This is often the way it is. Take the compulsory arbitration matter last year. Most of the people don't have the vaguest notion about this, but the labor groups will notice and take account of it. (32)

This research is important because it supports the view that voters need not be generally attentive to political issues in order to ensure accountability. As long as voters are informed about the issues they care about, they are likely to hold members of Congress accountable when they are not responsive. Moreover, as long as members of Congress recognize this, they will have an incentive to anticipate such reactions and act to defuse them by voting in line with the preferences of attentive— and politically significant—publics.

The notion that when citizens are interested in politics they will also learn more about politics is a simple and compelling idea. Unfortunately, support for this thesis has not always been overwhelming. Although many scholars do find support for this hypothesis (Iyengar 1990; Hutchings 2001; Krosnick 1988, 1990b; Krosnick et al. 1994; Popkin 1991; Repass 1971), others do not (Margolis 1977; Niemi and Bartels 1985; Nueman 1986; Price and Zaller 1993; Rabinowitz, Prothro, and Jacoby 1982; Wolpert and Gimpel 1997).[6] Why does evidence of issue salience emerge under some circumstances but not others? One explanation for the mixed findings is that previous efforts to study issue publics have typically not considered contextual factors.

Forces outside of the individual also play a critical role in the process of voter monitoring. More specifically, contextual factors such as the level of media coverage devoted to a legislator's position on various issues and the manner in which those issues are covered can also influence citizen engagement in politics. These considerations are important because they help to determine *when* heightened attentiveness should occur among issue publics. For example, Iyengar and Kinder (1987), along with others, have found that particular issues are more apt to influence political judgments when those issues are prominently covered in the media. This effect, referred to as "priming," is extremely robust and has been supported with both experimental and survey methodologies (Iyengar and Kinder 1987; Krosnick and Brannon 1993; Krosnick and Kinder 1990; Mendelberg 2001; Valentino, Hutchings, and White 2002).

The impact of priming on citizen engagement is considerable. Nevertheless, I believe that previous work may have underestimated the influence of these contextual factors. For one thing, the priming hypothesis was designed to identify media effects, and few subsequent elaborations have explicitly applied the theory to campaign settings.[7] This is significant because priming effects should also occur when candidates emphasize issues (albeit through the mass media). More importantly, however, scholars have not paid sufficient attention to the *joint effects* of contextual variables and measures of issue salience.[8] Both factors should have independent effects on voter monitoring, but their combined effects should be especially powerful.

The hypothesized relationship between context, motivation, voter monitoring, and political outcomes is summarized in figure 1.1. Perceptions of issue importance and contextual factors should have both direct (as indicated by the dotted lines) and interactive (as indicated by the solid line) effects on levels of political engagement. Further, the latter effects are likely to be stronger than the former effects. When these factors are present, interest in the political process should increase along

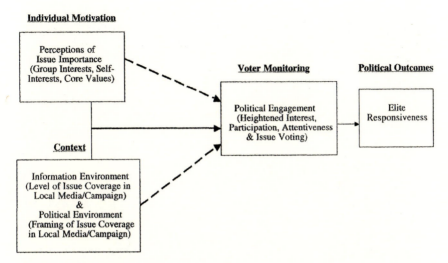

Figure 1.1. Hypothesized Relationships among Constituent Attitudes, Political Context, and Elite Responsiveness.

with information levels, issue voting, and participation rates. These forces should in turn influence policy decisions both because of politicians' anticipation of these effects (i.e., the impact of potential preferences) and through their direct influence on election outcomes.

This issue salience perspective on voting behavior fits comfortably with most of the models described above. For example, the aggregation model implicitly requires some small set of voters to actively monitor the political process. The issue salience theory identifies which voters are most likely to engage in this activity. The pressure group and potential preferences models undoubtedly provide a partial explanation for the relatively high levels of political responsiveness, but they are also incomplete. An issue salience perspective supplements these accounts by explaining why politicians are motivated to anticipate voter preferences or respond to the requests of interest group leaders. In both cases, successful politicians recognize that sometimes voters can be exceptionally attentive to politics, especially when their values or self-interests or group interests are threatened. In short, an emphasis on voter perceptions of issue importance clarifies our understanding of the relationship between public opinion and public policy. As the works of Fenno, Kingdon, and others have shown, legislators are generally convinced that some members of their constituencies do monitor their roll call votes. This perception is at odds with the bulk of public opinion research, unless one relies on the issue salience hypothesis.

Conclusion

The research cited above indicates that, while citizens may not monitor their representatives on every issue, voters are attentive to legislative activity on issues they perceive as important. This kind of voter oversight may not be routine, given the expectations of the potential preferences model, but it should predictably occur when certain conditions are present. To explore these conditions, this book will focus on the following research questions:

- Do the mass media provide sufficient information for voters to monitor their political representatives?
- When this information is provided, are the people most interested in the issue also more likely to learn about it?
- Do voters rely more on the issue they care about when casting their ballots? Under what circumstances does this occur?
- Do participation rates increase when issues voters care about are raised in campaigns?

The public opinion literature has clearly shown that, by most standards, the American electorate is generally uninformed about issues of public policy. At the same time, however, scholars have shown that politicians in general, and members of Congress in particular, adhere quite closely to the preferences of their constituents. Legislators are encouraged to be broadly responsive at least in part because they are convinced that the "wrong" vote (or set of votes) could prematurely end their career. On its face, this belief does not seem well founded, given what we know about the attentiveness of the average voter. I maintain that the gap in these findings can be bridged, in part, by paying greater attention to the issues voters care about. Such an emphasis takes into account the relative lack of interest among most citizens with regard to many issues of public policy yet still helps to explain why politicians are responsive.

That the public is often asleep does not mean that representatives can simply disregard their constituents' interests. On the contrary, the theme running throughout this book is that legislators are responsive to their constituents because of a *realistic* fear that interested voters can become informed and hold discrepant votes against them. It is true that part of the reason that citizen monitoring does not regularly occur is that voters do not often possess sufficient interest. However, the public is also inattentive to politics because their politicians do not typically behave in a way that departs from the expected. The ensuing chapters will show that when voters are unusually interested, and particularly when a politician's voting records or issue positions receive unusual coverage, voter monitoring can be considerable. Thus, the sleeping giants that make up public opinion may not often stir, but when they do politicians would be foolish to disregard them. More importantly, a wise representative will see to it that his or her constituents are not motivated to closely monitor legislative activities. The best way to accomplish this is by being responsive—at least on the issues significant voting blocs find important and are likely to find out about.

Finally, it should be noted that this book focuses entirely on the ways in which citizens react to the policy decisions of their elected, or prospective, representatives. Although the model summarized in figure 1.1 links these reactions, or the anticipation of them, to political outcomes, this step in the representation process is not directly explored here. However, two previous studies have confronted this issue. In the first (Hutchings 1998), I showed that, at least under some circumstances, legislators are concerned with the potential preferences of their constituents. Examining support among southern Democrats for the highly publicized 1990 Civil Rights Act, and an equally important yet obscure amendment to this legislation, I found that the size of the black constituency was a much more significant determinant of support for the 1990 act than for the amendment. This suggests that these typically moderate legislators are more likely to support expansive civil rights legislation when their African American constituents might learn of their vote.

In a follow-up piece (Hutchings, McClerking, and Charles 2000), the range of bills was broadened to include both civil rights-related and social welfare votes across three separate congresses. Consistent with the earlier work, we found that white southern Democrats with significant black constituencies were more likely to support "black interests" on votes that received more media coverage. These results provide some support for the contention that concern with voter monitoring can significantly affect legislative outcomes. In the following chapters, I explain why this concern is justified.

Two

Local Press Coverage of Congressional Roll Call Votes

IN ORDER for the public to perform their required task in a representative democracy, they must first be provided with sufficient information about their representatives' political activities. Although political challengers and interest group leaders play an important role in the process of informing the electorate, arguably the most important responsibility belongs to the mass media. This chapter examines how effectively the media perform this task. By focusing on a diverse selection of bills, I provide a rough assessment of the level of coverage devoted to information on the voting decisions of specific legislators. The factors associated with this coverage are also examined, with particular attention paid to discrepant votes (i.e., votes against one's party) and legislative leadership (i.e., sponsorship or co-sponsorship of legislation). The issue of media coverage of congressional roll call votes is examined with a content analysis of major metropolitan newspapers.

As we shall see, in some instances the media do provide the public with adequate information to hold members of Congress accountable. Under other circumstances, however, this coverage is anything but adequate.

Congress and the Mass Media

Although no one would deny the importance of the mass media to an informed electorate, there has been comparatively little scholarly research on the factors affecting press coverage of congressional votes. Most of the research on the media and Congress focuses on coverage of the institution or the influence that television in particular has had on the legislative process (Cook 1989). Research has also focused on identifying predictors of media coverage during the campaign season (Goldenberg and Traugott 1987; Kahn 1991, 1995; Kahn and Kenny 1999; Tidmarch, Hyman, and Sorkin 1984). Oftentimes the emphasis in this literature is on how much coverage is provided in competitive versus less competitive races, or among House members relative to senators, or incumbents relative to challengers, or members of Congress relative to governors and presidents (Kahn 1991, 1995; Squire and Fastnow 1994; Tidmarch, Hyman, and Sorkin 1984).

This literature is important, but, given our interest in legislative responsiveness, it suffers from at least two disadvantages. First, to my knowledge, no scholar has examined how much information is provided about the votes of specific members of Congress on specific roll call votes. In most cases, researchers simply determine how frequently a member of Congress's name is mentioned in connection with a particular issue or set of issues. Invariably, there is not a great deal of precision in determining the position of the member on a particular roll call or issue. Newspapers may indeed provide extensive information on a member's position on a general issue (e.g., health care, civil rights, or the economy). This may not, however, reflect how he or she voted on a specific piece of legislation. In at least some cases, it is conceivable that voters would want to know about their legislator's general voting patterns *and* their position on specific bills.

Second, an area scarcely addressed in the extant literature is information arising *outside* of the campaign season. Some psychological research suggests that voters can retain this information for later use at election time, especially if it is considered personally relevant (Fiorina 1981; Iyengar 1990; Lodge, McGraw, and Stroh 1989; Lodge, Steenbergen, and Brau 1995; also see chapter 3). This is important because, in many cases, information on the incumbent's record does not arise during the campaign, particularly in House races, which attract little media attention and frequently involve weak challengers (Jacobson 1992). For these reasons, this chapter focuses on roll call votes both in and outside of the campaign season.

If the media are to provide information assisting the electorate in their democratic duties, then, ideally, the press should regularly supply information on the important issue positions or voting records of incumbents in a timely manner. This does not generally occur according to some scholars (Graber 1993; Patterson 1994, Patterson and McClure 1976). Media coverage of legislators' issue positions does not normally occur even during an election campaign, unless the incumbent faces a strong challenger (Kahn and Kenney 1999). This lack of issue coverage can be attributed to the news media's incentive to cover politics in such a way as to gain viewers or sell newspapers. As a result, they pay little attention to "recurrent complex and mundane problems, such as Congressional reorganization or the annual farm bill" (Graber 1993: 293). The assumption among journalists is that these kinds of issues will not grab the attention of the average American, who has only passing interest in politics.

If the media are to be an effective watchdog on politicians, however, then they should at least devote attention to potentially controversial voting decisions. It is, after all, the media's role to alert the public when a member of Congress either takes a position that is unresponsive to his or her constituents or departs from the position of the national party *because* of a concern with being responsive to local concerns.[1] Typically, politicians vote in predictable ways for both ideological and electoral reasons (Arnold 1990; Hutchings, McClerking, and Charles 2000; Key 1961; Miller and Stokes 1963). When members of Congress venture outside these bounds, it is the responsibility of the media or other political elites to bring this information to the public's attention. Fortunately, this duty also coincides with the criteria the media use to determine whether or not a story is newsworthy (Graber 1993; Patterson 1994). Thus, although the press does not routinely report on the voting activities of members of Congress (particularly on less prominent votes), it may have a financial incentive to provide coverage when an individual takes a position that is unusual or noteworthy.

My expectation is that when members vote contrary to local opinion or when they take an unusually active leadership role on behalf of their constituents, they will also receive more prominent media coverage. This should be especially true for less important legislation. This is because information on the votes of specific members should be provided on the more consequential roll calls regardless of how predictable the vote was. If press coverage does not vary in this way, then it may still be possible that public opinion is activated in the ways outlined in figure 1.1. However, this effect would be more dependent on the actions of interest group leaders and political challengers than on the independent reporting of the news media. Given the resource constraints of these actors relative to those of the press, this would also suggest that the electorate is less likely to become politically engaged. Nor could they be fairly blamed for their ignorance. The aim of this chapter, then, is to determine both the extent of local press coverage of roll call votes and, more importantly, the conditions under which it supplies the public with information necessary for effective monitoring.

Determining the Political Significance of Congressional Votes

As indicated at the outset of this chapter, the political significance of a particular vote is likely to affect the level of media coverage it receives. This is hardly a controversial contention. However, how does one determine whether or not a vote is indeed politically significant? As it turns out, a number of publications that report specifically on the activities of Congress identify so-called key votes in every legislative session. One of the most respected is the *Congressional Quarterly Almanac*. I relied on this source in selecting bills that professional observers of Congress considered politically significant.[2]

The specific key votes selected in this chapter are the Use of Force Resolution for the Persian Gulf War, the 1995 effort to pass the Balanced Budget Amendment to the Constitution, the confirmation vote of Clarence Thomas to the U.S. Supreme Court, the 1990 Civil Rights Bill, the 1992 Family Leave Act, and the 1988 Plant Closing Notification Bill.[3] Routine votes were selected based on the criteria that they are of particular concern to various issue publics but less important to most Americans and hence not politically significant to most members of Congress. The selection of these votes relied heavily on the voting scores compiled in each session of Congress by two interest groups. These scores identify votes of special concern to the groups and determine where members of Congress stand on their issues. The interest groups relied upon in this chapter are the American Federation of Labor and Congress of Industrial Organizations (AFL-CIO) and the Leadership Conference on Civil Rights (LCCR). Two votes were drawn from each of the interest groups.[4] The four examples of routine votes are the 1995 cloture vote in the Senate on President Clinton's striker replacement policy, the 1992 confirmation vote of Edward Carnes, Jr., to the Eleventh Circuit Court of Appeals, the extension of unemployment benefits in 1993, and a GOP amendment to the 1990 Civil Rights Bill. While probably unimportant to most Americans and not rated as key votes by *Congressional Quarterly Almanac*, these four votes were important to organized labor and civil rights groups.

I make no claim that these ten roll calls are a representative sample of congressional votes; taken as a group, they are clearly more prominent than a strictly representative sample. Indeed, even the routine votes are likely to be viewed by the media as considerably more important than standard congressional action on local projects or obscure budget items. My bias toward more prominent pieces of legislation is unlikely to undermine the objectives of this chapter. While it may understate the difference in levels of coverage between key votes and more routine legislation, it should not affect my interest in identifying the predictors of this coverage. At best, it limits my ability to generalize to especially obscure roll calls.

In order to measure media coverage of these votes, major metropolitan newspapers were examined in approximately two dozen states in the week following each roll call.[5] In most cases, the papers with the largest circulation were selected so as to focus on coverage with the greatest potential impact on the local population.[6] The vote on the confirmation of Supreme Court nominee Clarence Thomas is explored in some detail in chapter 3, whereas the Gulf War Use of Force Resolution received extensive coverage in the media and so detailed explanations are unnecessary here. The remaining votes require a little more exposition and are described briefly in the appendix to this chapter.

Measuring Media Coverage of Congressional Votes

The type of press coverage a bill receives has two major dimensions: whether it is reported at all; and, if reported on, the prominence of the coverage. To capture these elements, a 5-point scale was designed to measure levels of media prominence. The following list presents the coding scheme in detail.

CODING SCHEME FOR MEDIA COVERAGE OF
CONGRESSIONAL ROLL CALL VOTES

1. *Front Page, Headline Story.* Member of Congress is either mentioned in a "How They Voted" chart appearing on the front page **or** the subject of front-page story headline. **(4)**

2. *Front Page Story, Mention.* Member of Congress is mentioned in portion of front-page story that actually appears on front page (defined as first ten paragraphs), but not in the headline or a "How They Voted" chart. **(3)**

3. *How They Voted.* Member of Congress is mentioned in chart displayed on the **inside** of the newspaper. **(2)**

4. *Inside Mention.* Member of Congress is mentioned in text of a story appearing on a page other than the front page. This includes stories where the specific votes of the local party delegation are not reported but the party breakdown is reported. For example, a paper might report that all of the state's Republicans supported some measure and all of the Democrats opposed it. **(1)**

5. *No Mention.* No mention is made of how the state delegation voted. **(0)**

To receive the highest score, a 4, required a headline specifically referencing the vote of at least one member of Congress (typically a senator) in the local or state delegation. For example, a front-page headline story on the 1990 Civil Rights Bill in the *Louisville Courier-Journal* read "McConnell Blasted for Rights Bill Vote." This story went on to mention in the first sentence how both Kentucky senators voted on this bill. The *Chicago Tribune's* coverage of the Thomas confirmation is another example of a story coded 4. Although there was no headline story specifically mentioning the vote of the local Senate delegation, the *Tribune* provided a "How They Voted Chart" on the front page that listed the votes of all regional senators. Just below front-page headline stories are articles in

TABLE 2.1
Content Analysis of News Coverage of Legislation in the Week Following
Congressional Action

	Prominence			% Newspapers	Number of
	Median	High	Low	Mentioning	Newspapers
Key votes					
Thomas nomination (Senate)	2	4	0.5	100	25
Balanced budget '95 (Senate)	2	4	1	100	26
Balanced budget '95 (House)	2	3	0	93	26
Gulf War (Senate)	2	4	1	100	24
Gulf War (House)	2	4	0	96	24
Civil rights, final vote (Senate)	2	4	1	100	24
Civil rights, final vote (House)	2	3	0	87	24
Family leave '92 (Senate)	2	3	0	88	25
Family leave '92 (House)	2	3	0	92	25
Plant closing (Senate)	2	3	0	91	22
Plant closing (House)	1	2	0	67	21
Routine votes					
Striker (Senate)	0.5	1	0	50	26
Carnes nomination (Senate)	1	3	0	61	26
Civil rights (House)	0	3	0	29	24
Unemployment benefits (House)	0	2	0	39	23

Source: Courtesy of LexisNexis and Westlaw.
Note: Values range from 0 to 4 with higher values indicating more prominent media coverage.

which the votes of the state's congressional delegation are mentioned in
the text of the front-page story but not given special emphasis. Additionally, these mentions had to occur in the portion of the article that actually
appeared on the front page of the newspaper. These stories were coded
3.[7] "How They Voted Charts" appearing on the inside of the paper were
coded 2. The remaining values in the coding scheme were all determined very easily. Articles mentioning individual members' votes in the
text of stories on the inside of the newspaper received a 1, whereas articles that made no reference to how the local delegation voted were
coded 0.

Table 2.1 shows the median level of prominence, high and low values,
as well as the percentage of papers providing any coverage for each of
the ten bills in both the Senate and the House.[8] As can be seen, the level
of prominence given to a roll call vote varies considerably among the ten
cases. As expected, the key votes in this study were more prominently
covered than the more routine votes. For example, 100 percent of the
newspapers in this sample reported on the individual votes of senators

on the Gulf War and Clarence Thomas roll calls. Somewhat less coverage was accorded to the family leave and the plant closing roll calls. Alternatively, less than two-thirds of the newspapers in this content analysis gave any indication at all of how senators voted on the Carnes vote, and only half reported on the votes for the striker replacement. The routine House votes in this sample received even less coverage. Slightly more than one-third of the newspapers in my sample reported the votes of House members on the extension of unemployment benefits, and only 29 percent did so for the amendment to the Civil Rights Bill. Moreover, these routine votes probably received better coverage than most bills of this type because major interest groups (e.g., the AFL-CIO and the LCCR) considered these roll calls especially important. Standard legislation not targeted by major interest groups would undoubtedly receive far less coverage.

Another noteworthy finding is that the newspapers almost always provided more prominent information for the Senate votes than for the House votes. The one exception to this pattern is the coverage of local House member votes on the family leave legislation. This particular House vote may have received greater attention because the Senate had earlier voted to override President Bush's veto for the first time, only to have the House sustain the veto by twenty-seven votes.[9]

This overall trend is consistent with other observations that the news media generally give lower priority to House members (Graber 1993; Jacobson 1992). A more precise appreciation for the differences between the votes can be achieved by comparing the distributions of roll call votes of varying levels of importance. Figure 2.1 shows the type of coverage received for three votes of varying levels of prominence. One, the Thomas confirmation vote, received exceptionally heavy coverage, whereas another key vote—the Family Leave Act—received somewhat lesser coverage. The third vote, the Carnes vote, was viewed as more routine.[10]

Clearly, coverage varies greatly across these three cases. Of the three, the Thomas confirmation vote was the only one to receive front-page, headline coverage. Moreover, the modal level of coverage was a "How They Voted" chart attached to the story that would be difficult for even the most casual reader to miss. Finally, every newspaper in the sample reported the votes of their members of Congress on this roll call. Thus, in the case of truly exceptional key votes, such as the Thomas confirmation, interested voters are supplied with ample opportunity to learn the position of their senator.

The family leave legislation, however, presents a somewhat different picture. Although, the *Congressional Quarterly Almanac*, also considered this roll call to be a key vote, there were no (front-page) headline stories, and slightly more than 10 percent did not report the information at all.

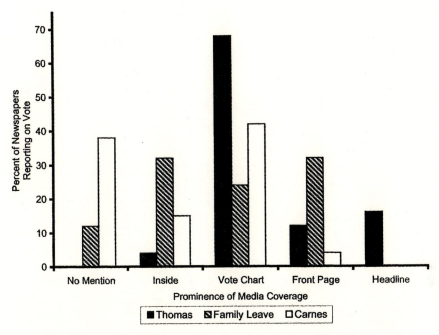

Figure 2.1. Levels of Media Prominence for Selected Senate Votes. (Courtesy of LexisNexis and Westlaw)

About a third of the papers in my sample did report the votes of the local senators on the front page, but just as many included the information within stories located inside the newspaper. In many cases, these mentions were buried near the bottom of the story. Casual readers would undoubtedly have a more difficult time learning how their senators voted on legislation of this kind.

The Carnes confirmation represents yet another type of vote. These votes, although important to particular groups, are often invisible to a large fraction of newspaper readers. Contrast this vote with coverage on the Thomas confirmation. Both involved a controversial nominee to the federal court, yet the Carnes vote was scarcely mentioned on the front pages at all, while a quarter of the newspapers in my sample reported the Thomas vote on the front page. Similarly, with the Carnes vote, almost 40 percent of the newspapers in my sample provide no mention of how the local senators voted, if indeed the story was reported at all.

A very similar pattern holds for House votes as shown in figure 2.2. As with the Thomas vote, the momentous Gulf War vote is the only one of the three that received front-page, headline coverage, and almost two-thirds of the newspapers in the sample displayed the votes in an easily

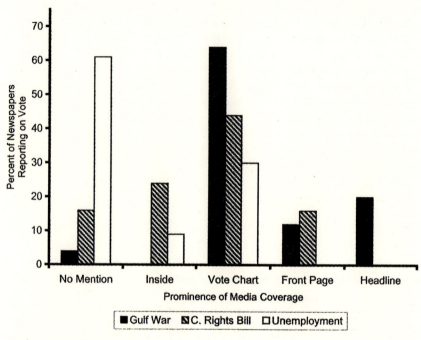

Figure 2.2. Levels of Media Prominence for Selected House Votes. (Courtesy of LexisNexis and Westlaw)

discernible "How They Voted" chart. In contrast, the controversial 1990 Civil Rights Bill and the vote on extension of unemployment benefits were far less prominently covered.

Perhaps it is unreasonable to expect that newspapers would devote a significant share of their resources to covering the activities of the local congressional delegation in Washington. Clearly, they cannot be expected to report on every bill that comes before Congress. Still, it would not require much additional effort for papers that in most cases already report the overall vote on many important bills also to include information on the votes of local members of Congress. As we have seen with routine pieces of legislation, particularly in the House of Representatives, this is not often done.

Predicting Media Coverage of Congressional Votes

At least three variables may plausibly influence the level of coverage devoted to a particular roll call. The first of these is the newspaper's circulation.[11] Studies have found circulation rates to be significantly related to campaign coverage in both the House and Senate (Tidmarch, Hyman, and Sorkin 1984). That is, larger papers devote less space than smaller newspapers to members of Congress during their reelection campaigns. This may be because some papers with especially large circulations, such as the *Los Angeles Times*, the *Washington Post*, and the *New York Times*, also serve national as well as local audiences. If this finding holds for reporting on roll call votes, then larger newspapers should allocate less prominent coverage to their congressional delegations than smaller papers such as the *Anchorage Daily News*, the *Providence Journal-Bulletin*, or the *Wichita Eagle*.

Factors specific to the individual legislator may also influence media coverage. One such factor is whether or not one or more members of the local congressional delegation voted against the position taken by the majority of fellow party members.[12] As described above, these are among the votes about which constituents should be most informed since they represent an act of either unusual responsiveness or nonresponsiveness.[13] Another way of measuring the local political environment is by identifying whether a member of the local delegation took a position of leadership on behalf of, or in opposition to, a specific piece of legislation. For example, Senator Edward Kennedy (D-MA) and Representative Augustos Hawkins (D-CA) were the chief sponsors of the 1990 Civil Rights Bill. If local factors of this kind are important, then media coverage of the Civil Rights Bill should have been particularly prominent in these two states.[14] This variable is coded as 1 when members of Congress are described in *Congressional Quarterly Weekly Report* as being linked in some way to the legislation or as taking a leadership role and coded as 0 for all other members.

The effects of the explanatory variables are determined separately for House members and senators. This is done because the factors influencing media coverage may work differently in the two chambers. In both cases, the results were obtained with ordered logistic regression analysis, as reported in the appendix to this chapter.[15] Let us first examine the results for the Senate votes. Figures 2.3 and 2.4 show the impact of a senator's opposition to his or her party's position, or his or her leadership role on a specific bill, on the level of media prominence devoted to coverage of the vote.[16] The circulation of the newspaper had no effect on this coverage, and its effects in the model are held constant at its median value.

Figure 2.3 presents the results of the antiparty vote variable for key bills. Whether or not one of the senators voted against the national party's position, newspapers provided excellent coverage of the vote. However, when at least one senator defied the national party, newspapers were more likely to provide *prominent* coverage of the vote. These effects are not dramatic, but they do run in the expected direction. For exam-

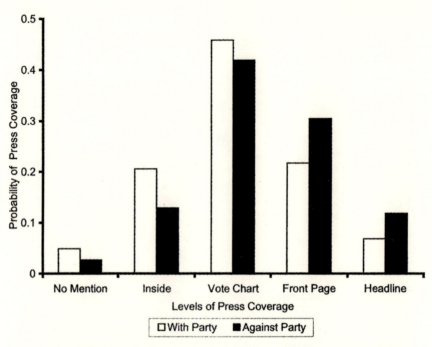

Figure 2.3. Predicted Probability of Press Coverage for Key Senate Votes, by Support for or Opposition to Party Vote. Probabilities are based on ordered logistic regression analyses in table 2A.

ple, headline mentions on the front-page increase from a probability of .07 to a probability of .12 for key votes. The probability of information on the senator's specific vote being mentioned on the front page at all is about .29 when he or she votes as expected but increases to .42 when at least one senator disagrees with the position of the national party.

The effect of the antiparty vote variable is even greater for less prominent votes, as shown in figure 2.4. Here we see that voting against the party affects both the quantity *and* the quality of media coverage. When senators vote in the manner expected of them, over half of the newspapers in my sample provide no information on their vote. However, when an unexpected vote is cast, the probability of receiving no coverage declines to about .15. Even when senators vote against their party on routine votes, they are not likely to get covered on the front page. Still, the probability that a newspaper will provide information on the vote in a chart on the inside of the paper is about .36 compared to a probability of .10 when senators vote with their party. This represents a rather impressive difference in press coverage.

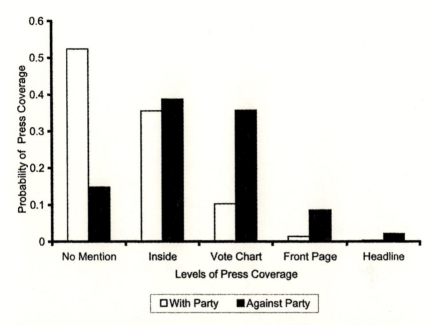

Figure 2.4. Predicted Probability of Press Coverage for Routine Senate Votes, by Support for or Opposition to Party Vote. Probabilities are based on logistic regression analyses in table 2A.

The effects of legislative leadership are also quite large, but only for routine votes, as shown in figure 2.5.[17] Whether or not a local senator was a leading supporter or critic of a bill has essentially no effect on coverage of more prominent votes (see appendix table 2A). When a senator is a strong backer or opponent of a vote, the probability that the local press will *not* provide information about their vote is about .27. When specific senators are not associated with a vote in this way, the corresponding probability is .52. Of course, as these votes are relatively obscure, legislative leadership rarely results in front-page headline stories. However, this variable does increase the probability of the vote being displayed in a "How They Voted" chart. This probability is only .10 in the absence of legislative leadership, but .24 when senators are more active.

Turning now to the House, we find that neither voting against one's party nor legislative leadership has a significant effect on the level of press coverage provided (see appendix table 2B). If anything, these variables have a slightly negative effect. There was some tendency for results to move in the opposite direction for more routine votes, but these effects fell well short of conventional levels of statistical significance. We

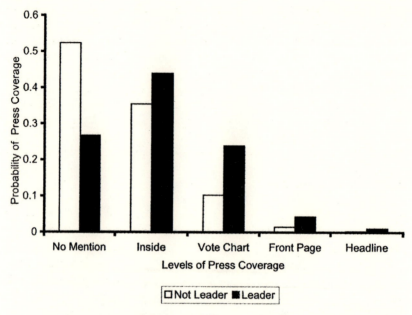

Figure 2.5. Predicted Probability of Press Coverage for Routine Senate Votes, by Legislative Leadership. Probabilities are based on logistic regression analyses in table 2A.

know from table 2.1 that newspapers do provide information on the votes of individual House members, at least on politically significant bills. However, there is no evidence that this coverage is contingent on factors that might facilitate voter monitoring.

Conclusion

Citizens need not routinely follow political matters if they are to hold their elected leaders accountable. However, they do need to know when their representatives are not responsive to their wishes. Additionally, citizens should presumably also know when members of Congress are unusually active on their behalf. The principal aim of this chapter was to determine whether or not the media provide this information.

Overall, the results were mixed. In the case of Senate votes, I found that the mass media (or at least daily newspapers) performed adequately.[18] As one might expect, the more politically important votes generated more thorough and more prominent news coverage. Regardless of the importance of the vote, however, when at least one senator voted against the wishes of his or her party, newspapers were more likely to bring this to the attention of their readers. This was especially true of less important votes. This latter conclusion is somewhat tentative given that only two votes were examined in the Senate. However, because the same general pattern emerged across each type of vote, it seems likely that this variable does indeed matter. Additionally, assuming a leadership role on a particular vote was also a strong predictor of increased media coverage for routine votes, but not for key pieces of legislation. This latter finding may be explained, in part, by the fact that there was already little room for improved coverage among the more prominent votes. In any case, these results indicate that the public does receive sufficient information to hold their senators accountable.

At first glance, this conclusion appears to run counter to the findings of Graber (1993), Patterson (1994), and Kahn and Kenny (1999).[19] These scholars find little evidence of media scrutiny of legislators' issue positions. The results of this chapter are not incompatible with this position. I also find that oftentimes, particularly on low-profile votes, the media do not provide much coverage of individual members' roll call votes. However, most of the time they do not have to provide this information because legislators vote in thoroughly predictable ways. The responsibility of the media comes primarily when members of Congress do *not* behave as expected. When this occurs, senators' votes are given more prominent coverage.

The strong relationships among legislative leadership, antiparty votes, and media coverage of congressional roll calls did not hold for House members. In general, the actions of local representatives had no effect on the amount of media coverage devoted to their voting behavior. This suggests that constituents wishing to learn about the activities of their representative will have to rely more heavily on other elites, such as political challengers or interest group leaders, to provide the necessary information. Clearly, these actors *can* perform this task (Kollman 1998; Zaller 1996). Unfortunately, given the resource limitations of most interest groups and the relative infrequency of strong challengers in House races, it is unclear how frequently they *do* perform this function.

*Appendix to Chapter 2*_____

Description of Roll Call Votes

Selected Key Votes

THE 1995 Balanced Budget Amendment called for a balanced budget by
2002 or the second fiscal year after the amendment was ratified by the
states. Congress could waive this requirement if three-fifths of the House
and Senate voted in favor of deficit spending, or if a simple majority ap-
proved such a measure during wartime or when the national security was
threatened. Additionally, the amendment would prevent the courts from
ordering tax increases or spending cuts without congressional approval.

The Civil Rights Bill of 1990 was one of the most important pieces of
legislation for the civil rights community in several years. The law was
designed to reverse or modify six recent Supreme Court decisions that
had limited the scope and remedies of job discrimination laws. After
eight months of bitter negotiations between Congress and the White
House, President Bush ultimately vetoed the legislation. The Senate
failed to override Bush's veto by one vote.

The Plant Closing Notification Bill required that companies with more
than one hundred employees give sixty days' notice before they could
fire or lay off their workers. Initially it was presented as part of an omni-
bus trade bill that was vetoed by President Reagan. The Senate later removed the plant-closing language from the trade legislation and submit-
ted it as a separate bill that attracted sufficient Republican support to
override another presidential veto. This vote was arguably the most important legislative priority for organized labor in 1988.

Finally, the 1992 Family Leave Act had been introduced several times
over the years only to either fail to muster enough votes or to face a
presidential veto. This legislation sought to allow employees up to twelve
weeks of unpaid leave from work in order to care for children or sick
family members. In 1992 the measure passed once again, only to be vetoed by President Bush. The Senate successfully overrode the veto, mark-
ing the first time such an event had occurred during the Bush administration. The House, however, later sustained the veto.

Routine Votes

The striker replacement vote was an effort on the part of Republicans in
the Senate to prevent President Clinton from implementing a recent

executive order that prevented some employers from permanently replacing striking workers. The Republican majority (with some Democratic votes) was unable to break a Democratic filibuster. Organized labor had tried, without success, in several previous Congresses to pass legislation that would have outlawed this practice.

The confirmation of Edward Carnes, Jr., to the Eleventh U.S. Circuit Court of Appeals had been delayed by opponents for eight months before finally coming to a vote. Most civil rights organizations strongly opposed the nomination. Critics argued that Carnes, an attorney general from Alabama, had supported (or at least not objected to) efforts by prosecutors to remove African American jurors in death penalty cases. Carnes was eventually confirmed, largely because of the support he received from Alabama's two Democratic senators, Howard Heflin and Richard Shelby.

The 1993 extension of unemployment benefits was an effort to continue a program, begun in 1991, that had extended federal unemployment benefits to workers whose access to state benefits had expired. Organized labor considered this bill a major issue, and it was eventually signed into law by President Clinton.

Table 2A

Ordered Logistic Regression Models Predicting News Coverage of Senators' Vote on Selected Roll Calls

	Regression Coefficient	*Standard Error*
Routine vote	−3.06***	0.42
Antiparty vote	0.61**	0.35
Local connection	−0.42	0.44
Circulation	0.002	0.005
Routine × Antiparty vote	1.23**	0.72
Routine × Local connection	1.53*	1.01
Cut 1	−2.90	0.39
Cut 2	−2.78	0.38
Cut 3	−1.00	0.30
Cut 4	−0.95	0.30
Cut 5	0.98	0.31
Cut 6	2.68	0.40
Pseudo R-square	0.12	
Log likelihood	−271.3638	
N	199	

* $p \leq .10$; ** $p < .05$; *** $p < .01$ for one-tailed test.

Table 2B

Ordered Logistic Regression Models Predicting News Coverage of
House Members' Vote on Selected Roll Calls

	Regression Coefficient	Standard Error
Routine vote	−2.54***	0.38
Antiparty vote	−0.01	0.30
Local connection	−0.50	0.45
Circulation	−0.01	0.01
Cut 1	−2.36	0.38
Cut 2	−1.17	0.34
Cut 3	1.00	0.35
Cut 4	2.69	0.53
Pseudo R square	0.18	
Log likelihood	−193.56009	
N	170	

$* \ p \leq .10; ** \ p < .05; *** \ p < .01$ for one-tailed test.

Table 2C

Newspaper Circulation

Newspapers	Circulation
1. Anchorage Daily News	60,086
2. Arizona Republic	445,214
3. Los Angeles Times	1,169,066
4. Denver Post	263,720
5. Hartford Courant	230,425
6. Miami Herald	400,336
7. Atlanta Journal and Const.	494,556
8. Chicago Tribune	721,556
9. Wichita Eagle	117,878
10. Louisville Courier-Journal (Kentucky)	235,144
11. New Orleans Times Picayune	266,592
12. Washington Post	810,904
13. Boston Globe	503,578
14. Detroit Free Press	598,418
15. Minneapolis Star Tribune	408,869
16. St. Louis Post Dispatch	369,005
17. New York Times	746,924
18. Charlotte Observer	230,883
19. Columbus Dispatch (Ohio)	261,086
20. Portland Oregonian	335,758
21. Philadelphia Inquirer	500,733
22. Providence Journal-Bull. (Rhode Is.)	196,118
23. Columbia State (South Carolina)	134,560
24. Memphis Comm. Appeal	193,211
25. Houston Post	292,061
26. Seattle Times	238,176

Three

Context, Motivation, and Selective Attentiveness to the Clarence Thomas Confirmation Vote

WE LEARNED in chapter 2 that, at least for senators, the mass media provide the necessary information for the public to learn how individual legislators voted on important bills. But who pays attention to this information when it is made available? As indicated in figure 1.1, perceptions of issue importance should play a significant role in determining who is attentive to political information and who is not. This chapter provides the first test of this hypothesis by focusing on attentiveness to a single high-profile vote in the U.S. Senate: the vote to confirm Clarence Thomas to the Supreme Court. If the issue salience theory is correct, then citizens particularly interested in the Thomas nomination should have been more informed about their senators' vote on this issue.

There are a number of ways of assessing which citizens were especially interested in the Thomas vote. The most obvious, of course, would be to simply ask them. Unfortunately, the surveys relied upon for this book did not ask this question. As indicated in the first chapter, however, researchers have identified the likely *sources* of attitude importance (Berelson, Lazarsfeld, and McPhee 1954; Boninger, Krosnick, and Berent 1995; Campbell et al. 1960; Key 1961; Popkin et al. 1976; Rokeach 1968, 1973; Yeric and Todd 1996). Typically, these attitudes are thought to emerge from either concerns about one's self-interest, group interest, or core values.[1] With this information, we can fashion indirect measures of these perceptions based on the demographic characteristics of the respondents, their social group memberships, or their response to value-laden survey questions. In the case of the Thomas vote, as will shortly become apparent, this suggests we focus on gender (as a means of getting at self-interests and perhaps group interest), racial group membership (as a measure of group interest), and ideology (as a determinant of the role of core values).

Previous efforts to adopt this strategy of measuring perceptions of issue salience, both with regard to the Thomas vote and more generally, have not always resulted in strong support for the issue salience theory (see, for example, Price and Zaller 1993; Wolpert and Gimpel 1997). Part of the explanation for this may lie in the precision with which indirect measures of issue salience were constructed. Instead of focusing merely on women, blacks, and ideologues, this chapter will adopt a more nuanced approach. For example, the issues raised during the Thomas hearings were just as likely to be salient to some men as they were to some women. As argued more fully below, liberal women and conservative men should have been particularly interested in the outcome of the vote.

In addition to individual-level differences, citizens also encountered important differences in their informational and political environments that should have affected knowledge of this vote. One example of the potential importance of the informational environment is the senators' varying electoral status. Some senators faced reelection roughly one year after the Thomas vote and encountered challengers who would campaign on the issue. Also, there were more than just differences regarding the *quantity* of information that was made available on this vote. The *quality* of political information also differed across political jurisdictions. Specifically, the political stakes surrounding this vote were much higher for some senators than for others. It is possible, therefore, that the political environment provided an additional incentive for constituents to learn whether or not their senator supported the nomination. Moreover, individual perceptions of issue salience should interact with cues in the political environment to bolster citizen information levels.

Finally, this examination of the Thomas vote can help to shed light on an important debate on the acquisition of political information. If attentiveness is confined to a small group of voters with a general appetite for political news, then the politically sophisticated should be most informed about the Thomas vote (Delli Carpini and Keeter 1996; Price and Zaller 1993; Zaller 1992). If, however, political knowledge varies from one issue to the next, then those individuals with a particular interest in the Thomas vote should be more familiar with their senators' vote on this issue.

The Politics of the Thomas Nomination

Before discussing the factors that predict attentiveness to the Thomas confirmation vote, it is first necessary to provide some background on the extraordinary circumstances surrounding that vote. From the beginning, the nomination of Clarence Thomas was an unusual event because it was infused with racial symbolism. This was partially due to Thomas's race. He remains only the second African American, following the venerable Thurgood Marshall, to be nominated for a seat on the Supreme Court. Issues of race also took center stage, however, because of conscious efforts on the part of the Bush administration to deflect criticism from the nomination by highlighting Thomas's impressive efforts to rise above his impoverished background. In this vein, the *Houston Chronicle* described Thomas as a man who began the confirmation process as someone "with the image of an impoverished child of the segregated South who rose to federal power in Washington."[2]

Unlike most presidential nominees, Thomas was not assured of his confirmation in the Democrat-controlled Senate. At forty-three, he had a rather brief and undistinguished record on the federal bench. More importantly, as a staunch conservative replacing the defiantly liberal Marshall, Thomas would solidify an already conservative majority on the Supreme Court. Some senators also publicly questioned his assertion that he had never discussed the *Roe v. Wade* decision that legalized abortion.[3] Nevertheless, although the Senate Judiciary Committee deadlocked on their recommendation of Thomas in late September 1991, the nomination was scheduled to go before the full Senate. The weekend before the vote, however, an allegation surfaced in the press that Thomas had sexually harassed one of his assistants when he worked in the Department of Education and at the Equal Employment Opportunity Commission. Thomas denied the charge that he had repeatedly made unwelcome sexual advances toward his then subordinate, Oklahoma law professor Anita Hill. Nevertheless, the vote was postponed and a new round of public hearings was scheduled to address the charges.

Predictably, most liberal groups and civil rights organizations opposed the nomination. Surprisingly, however, black citizens remained supportive of Thomas. In fact, support among blacks actually increased after Professor Hill accused Thomas of sexual harassment (Caldeira and Smith 1996). Before the charges were raised, support for Thomas among blacks and whites was about 55 percent, according to the *Los Angeles Times*. A few days before the confirmation vote, however, support for Thomas reached 61 percent among blacks compared with 50 percent among whites.[4] Thomas and the Bush administration were effective in rallying black support in part because, ironically, their defense relied heavily on racial imagery. In the most celebrated example, Thomas referred to his questioning by the all-white Senate judiciary committee as a "high-tech lynching for uppity blacks."[5]

This strategy not only solidified Thomas's support among the black masses but also led to divisions among black elites. For example, although the national NAACP opposed the nomination, several local branches supported it. These included branches in East St. Louis and Compton, which sent representatives to Washington, DC, to testify on Thomas's behalf (Pinderhughes 1992). Many local leaders of the NAACP also expressed ambivalence on the nomination and subsequent confirmation. For example, the *Columbus Dispatch* reported the conflicted response of a local leader in Ohio. "'His (legal) background is terrible,' said Sybil Edwards-McNabb, president of the Columbus chapter of the NAACP. Nevertheless, she said at the organization's Freedom Fund banquet at the Hyatt Regency Columbus, 'I am pleased' with the confirmation."[6] Finally, a surprising number of black elites came out in support of the nomination. These included Virginia Governor Douglas Wilder, Reverend Joseph Lowery of the Southern Christian Leadership Conference, President Niara Sudarkasa of Lincoln University, columnist William Raspberry, Harvard sociologist Orlando Patterson, and poet Maya Angelou (Burnham 1992; Marable 1992; Pinderhughes 1992).

Among women, reaction to the harassment charges, and to Thomas's subsequent defense, varied by ideology. For example, liberal women's groups strongly opposed Thomas. After Thomas was confirmed, the Women's Legal Defense Fund issued the following statement: "Today the Senate sacrificed the integrity of the Supreme Court, its own reputation, and the rights of American women to the Bush-Reagan agenda."[7] Other liberal women's organizations opposing the nomination included the National Women's Political Caucus, the National Organization of Women, the Fund for a Feminist Majority, and the National Abortion Rights Action League. Overall, however, public opinion polls taken at the time consistently showed that Thomas received far more support than opposition from women (white and black). A *Los Angeles Times* poll reported that 48 percent of women supported the nomination compared with 54 percent of men.[8] Moreover, every national poll showed that a majority of women believed Thomas's version of events rather than Professor Hill's.[9]

In spite of majority or near-majority support among men, women, blacks, and whites, the Thomas nomination was in serious trouble. The changing political landscape was most apparent among Democrats. After the first set of hearings, thirteen Democratic senators, more than enough to ensure confirmation, announced their support for Thomas. Most of these senators were from the South. After the charges of sexual harassment were made public, these thirteen so-called swing Democrats were publicly ambivalent about the nomination, particularly as its fate was widely viewed as resting in their hands.[10]

Once the second round of hearings was completed, many of the swing Democrats agonized over their decision and sought advice from family and co-workers. For example, Senator Joseph Lieberman (CT) decided to oppose the nomination only after speaking with his twenty-two-year-old daughter. He described the vote as the most difficult he had cast in his three years in the Senate. Senator Richard Bryan (NV) said, "in 25 years, this is the toughest vote I've had to cast."[11] He received more calls from his constituents on this matter than on the Persian Gulf War, with most favoring Judge Thomas.

Although some swing Democrats were concerned about how female staff or family members would react to the vote, many more were concerned with how their black constituents would respond. This was especially true in the South. For example, the *Charlotte Observer* noted the following:

> While some female leaders were expressing disappointment with Hollings (D-SC) for his pro-Thomas stance, he was receiving support from another important political group—the state's elected black officials. Many were warm in their praise of the senator for sticking by the nominee. "It was the right thing to do," said state Sen. Herbert Fielding, D-Charleston, chairman of the Legislative Black Caucus. Feminists who opposed Thomas's nomination said they were not a potent political force in South Carolina to compete with black constituents for Hollings's support.[12]

Both journalists and political scientists believed that swing Democrats with large African American constituencies provided Thomas with his margin of victory (Overby et al. 1992). In fact, some journalists argued that the Bush administration shrewdly used black support for Thomas to pressure these ambivalent Democrats. The *New Orleans Times Picayune* described the political situation in the South as follows: "In charging racism, Thomas appeared to gain support from black viewers—an important consideration for many of the swing Democratic senators because their states have large black populations. President Bush sought to put further pressure on the wavering Democrats [the day before the vote] by publicly thanking blacks for siding with Thomas."[13]

In the end, only three of the thirteen swing Democrats—senators Bryan (NE), Lieberman (CT), and Reid (NV)—voted against the nomination. None of the swing Democrats from the South switched his vote. Thomas was confirmed on October 15, 1991, with a 52–48 vote, the smallest margin of victory of any successful nominee in the twentieth century.

Issue Salience, the Political Environment, and the Thomas Nomination

The summary of the politics surrounding the Thomas vote in the previous section provides many clues about which citizens might have been especially attentive to the vote. The prominent discussion of race, gender, and ideology suggests that blacks, women, and ideologues would be particularly interested in the outcome of the confirmation process. Of course, citizens could belong to more than one of these groups. However, multiple memberships would not necessarily enhance salience effects, particularly if those memberships implied opposing positions on the Thomas vote. For example, an individual's identity as a woman might predispose her to be sympathetic to Professor Hill even as her conservative ideological identity would lead her to support the nominee. As the early Columbia and Michigan models found, conflicting group identities are associated with less accurate political perceptions, lower levels of political participation, and less interest in politics (Berelson, Lazarsfeld, and McPhee 1954; Campbell et al. 1960).

Research on the impact of conflicting identities suggests that we should simultaneously consider gender *and* ideology when we seek to identify who would be especially attentive to this vote. As liberal women would not be conflicted in their position on this issue, they should also be more informed. Alternatively, we should find much weaker salience effects among conservative women. Similarly, liberal men might also be conflicted. As men, they may have felt some sympathy for Thomas, yet as liberals they probably opposed him on most issues. This conflict might cause them to disengage from the process and not become invested in the outcome. Finally, conservative men should also demonstrate heightened attentiveness on the Thomas vote as they were inclined to feel little conflict on the issue. As men, they could sympathize with Thomas's predicament, and as conservatives they could enthusiastically endorse his policy priorities.

Additional contextual variables beyond the content of the vote may have also stimulated attentiveness. Previous research has shown that citizens are more informed on political matters in areas with heavier media coverage (Chaffee and Wilson 1977). Thus, citizens should have been more informed on the Thomas vote in states that provided greater media attention to the issue. Although the amount of press coverage probably did not vary much across states at the time of the vote, some citizens were more likely to be reminded of their senators' position during the 1992 campaign season. In particular, some of these senators faced female challengers who were especially outspoken on this vote (Cook, Thomas, and Wilcox 1994; Paolino 1995; Sapiro and Conover 1997).

The different political contexts each senator faced may also have contributed to knowledge of this vote. Specifically, the political implications of this vote were *qualitatively* different in states represented by swing Democrats. Throughout the latter stages of the nomination process, the media made it clear that the fate of the nomination rested with these thirteen senators. I therefore hypothesize that residents in these states would be especially attentive to their senators' vote because the political stakes surrounding it were higher there. This enhanced attentiveness should be even greater among the issue publics examined in this chapter. This is especially true of African Americans. These citizens represented Thomas's strongest backers, and they would likely interpret a vote against him as a threat to their group interest (Hutchings et al. 2001; Marcus and MacKuen 1993). This fact was not lost on swing Democrats. Recall that most of these legislators represented southern states with large black constituencies and could ill-afford to alienate these voters (Overby et al. 1992).

Information Generalists, Information Specialists, and the Political Environment

The data for my analyses are drawn from the 1992 portion of the Senate Election Study (SES).[14] This survey is useful for two reasons. First, it was designed to draw a random sample of roughly sixty respondents from each of the fifty states. Thus, comparisons can be made across states in a way that has rarely been possible before. Second, respondents were asked several questions about the Thomas hearings, including whether they supported the nomination at the time and how their senators voted.[15] Table 3.1 reports opinions on the Thomas nomination among various demographic groups.

At the time of the Thomas hearings, a number of national surveys indicated that, regardless of race, most Americans supported the nomination.[16] Additionally, there were no significant gender differences in the support for Thomas. The analyses in this chapter, however, are based on survey data drawn in the fall of 1992, over a year after Thomas was confirmed. Respondents were asked if they supported Thomas at the time of the confirmation vote, but it is possible that opinions may have shifted during that time and influenced recollections.

Even though the SES survey was conducted over a year after the vote, the 1992 results adhere closely to the results of other surveys conducted during the hearings. For example, the plurality of respondents indicated that they supported Thomas at the time of the confirmation vote. Also, even after a year of consistently conservative decisions on the Supreme Court, blacks were still more likely to support Thomas (or at least indicate that they had supported him) than were whites.[17] Unlike some of the surveys taken at the time, however, the SES survey finds that men were more supportive of Thomas than were women. Upon closer inspection, we find the effects of gender are contingent upon the race of the respondent. Among African Americans, there are no discernible gender differences in support for confirmation. Among whites, however, there is a significant difference, with women being less supportive.

How does ideology affect opinions on the nomination? I indicated near the beginning of this chapter that liberal men and conservative

Table 3.1
Attitudes toward the Thomas Nomination, by Gender, Race, and Ideology

	Support (%)	Opposed (%)	Don't Know (%)	N
Women	40	41	19	1,489
Men	50	34	16	1,270
Blacks	55	27	18	204
Women	56	27	17	119
Men	53	27	20	85
Whites	44	39	17	2,404
Women	39	43	18	1,308
Men	49	34	16	1,096
Ideology				
Liberals	33	54	13	676
Conservatives	54	28	18	1,292
Liberal women	30	58	11	369
Liberal men	37	48	15	307
Conservative women	49	30	20	660
Conservative men	60	25	15	632
All cases	45	38	17	

Source: 1988–1992 Senate Election Study.

women should be more divided in their attitudes about Thomas because of their conflicting group identities. If one merely examines liberals and conservatives (irrespective of gender), one finds, not surprisingly, that the former opposed Thomas and the latter supported him. Within each group, however, there were significant gender differences. As expected, the strongest opponents of Thomas were liberal *women*, and his strongest defenders were conservative *men*.

Table 3.2 reports the effects of the issue importance and contextual variables on knowledge of the Thomas vote.[18] Let us first turn our attention to gender differences. Even after statistically controlling for a variety of different variables related to political information, we find that men were more informed on this vote than were comparable women (see appendix to this chapter for description of control variables). The probability that women could identify the position of at least one of their senators on the Thomas vote was about .54. Among men, this probability was .63. This difference is not surprising given that women are generally less informed than men about national politics (Delli Carpini and Keeter 1996). As expected, however, these differences shift somewhat when we take into account ideology. Liberal women were more informed about their senators' vote on the Thomas nomination than were either liberal men or conservative women. Liberal women had a .68 probability of

Table 3.2
Predicted Probability of Identifying One or Both Senators'
Vote on the Thomas Confirmation, by Gender, Race,
Ideology, and Political Context

	None	One Senator	Both Senators
Gender			
Women	.46	.32	.22
Men	.37	.34	.29
Race			
Blacks	.49	.31	.20
Whites	.46	.32	.22
Ideology and gender			
Liberal women	.32	.34	.34
Liberal men	.41	.33	.26
Conservative women	.42	.33	.25
Conservative men	.29	.34	.37
Political context			
Blacks in swing states	.31	.34	.35
Whites in swing states	.44	.32	.23
Female candidate	.31	.34	.35
No female candidate	.46	.32	.22

Source: 1988–1992 Senate Election Study.
Note: Probabilities are based on logistic regression analyses presented in table 3A.

identifying the vote of at least one senator, whereas for liberal men and conservative women the probabilities were .59 and .58, respectively.[19]

An examination of ideological differences in attentiveness among men also conforms to expectation. Although, traditionally, liberal and conservative men do not differ on measures of general political knowledge, a difference clearly did emerge on the Thomas vote (Hutchings 2001). All else equal, conservative men had a .71 probability of identifying how at least one of their senators voted on the Thomas nomination. As indicated above, this result is almost 20 percent larger than the equivalent probability for liberal men.

Racial differences in knowledge of the Thomas vote also indicate the power of issue importance, albeit with a bit of a twist. Typically, blacks score much lower than whites on measures of general political information (Hutchings 2001). However, on the Thomas vote, this difference essentially disappears. Overall, the probability that blacks would accurately identify at least one senator's vote on the Thomas nomination was about .51 compared with .54 for whites. This racial gap is turned on its head in states represented by swing Democrats. The model predicts that the probability that an African American in these states would know the position of at least one of their senators was .69. The equivalent probability among comparable whites was only .55.

The effects of the other measure of the political environment were also generally consistent with expectations, although this context effect was not greater for blacks, liberal women, or conservative men. Underscoring the importance of the information environment, the presence of female Senate candidates had a significant and positive effect on knowledge levels, even after controlling for other important variables.[20] The average respondent in these states had a .69 probability of learning about the vote of at least one senator. When there were no female candidates in the race, this probability was only .54.

So far we have uncovered evidence supportive of the model laid out in figure 1.1. It is conceivable, however, that the individual and contextual variables associated with increased attentiveness to the Thomas vote would also be associated with any other roll call. To address this possibility, I also examined knowledge of the Gulf War vote. As we saw in chapter 2, this vote received at least as much coverage as the Thomas vote. The similarities end here, however, in that race and gender (although perhaps not ideology) were far less important to this vote than they were for the Thomas vote.

The relationship among our measures of salience, context, and the Gulf War vote are presented in table 3.3. Overall, accuracy rates are somewhat higher than those of table 3.2, but the salience and context effects are consistently weaker. Differences between liberal women and liberal men, for example, are essentially nil. Similarly, differences between conservative men and liberal men are also much smaller. The black-white gap in political knowledge is slightly greater on this vote, but, more importantly, the interaction of race and residence in a state with a swing Democrat is virtually zero. Finally, although the presence of female Senate candidates is associated with higher information levels on the Thomas vote, on the Gulf War vote this variable has no effect. As anticipated, measures of issue salience and context designed with the Thomas vote in mind do not easily translate to unrelated issues.[21]

We have established that, at least on the Thomas vote, issue publics were more likely to obtain political information than comparable citizens. However, how informed were individuals with more general interests in politics? Table 3.4 reports the results for these respondents. Recall that some scholars argue that information about specific political events can be best predicted by measures of general political interest. If this is true, then respondents who are generally informed about politics should have also known how their senators voted on the Thomas nomination and the Gulf War initiative. This theory is tested separately for men and women. As expected, respondents with high levels of general political

Table 3.3

Predicted Probability of Identifying One or Both Senators'
Vote on the Gulf War Use of Force, by Gender, Race,
Ideology, and Political Context

	None	One Senator	Both Senators
Gender			
Women	.28	.38	.34
Men	.17	.34	.49
Race			
Blacks	.35	.38	.27
Whites	.28	.38	.34
Ideology and gender			
Liberal women	.19	.35	.46
Liberal men	.19	.35	.46
Conservative women	.22	.37	.41
Conservative men	.15	.32	.53
Political context			
Blacks in swing states	.24	.37	.39
Whites in swing states	.25	.38	.37
Female candidate	.28	.38	.34
No female candidate	.28	.38	.34

Source: 1988–1992 Senate Election Study.
Note: Probabilities are based on logistic regression analyses
presented in table 3A.

knowledge also were more likely to learn about their senators' vote on
these specific roll calls. The effects of this variable are, however, about
twice as large for men as they are for women. Men who score low on the
political information scale had a .45 probability of identifying the position of at least one of their senators on the Thomas vote, but this rose
dramatically to .78 for men who score high on this scale.[22] For women,
the corresponding probabilities were only .46 and .62.

Issue Salience, the Political Environment, and the
1992 Senate Elections

Table 3.2 showed that issue salience and factors in the political environment can work both separately and interactively to increase political information levels. It seems likely, however, that the context effects would
be greater for senators whose term of office was up in 1992. This is, in
part, because six of the thirteen swing Democrats were up for reelection
that year, and this contributed to their anxiety regarding the Thomas
vote. Similarly, the female candidate variable should also be most

Table 3.4

Predicted Probability of Identifying One or Both Senators'
Vote on the Thomas Confirmation and Gulf War Use of
Force, by Gender and Level of Political Information

	Thomas Vote		
Political information	*None*	*One Senator*	*Both Senators*
Women, high	.38	.33	.28
Men, high	.22	.32	.46
Women, low	.54	.29	.17
Men, low	.55	.28	.16
	Gulf War Vote		
Political information	*None*	*One Senator*	*Both Senators*
Women, high	.23	.37	.40
Men, high	.09	.24	.67
Women, low	.31	.38	.30
Men, low	.27	.38	.35

Source: 1988–1992 Senate Election Study.

Note: Probabilities are based on logistic regression analyses presented in table 3A.

strongly associated with attentiveness to senators facing reelection. An
ideal way to test this proposition is to compare the effects of the contextual variables on senators up for reelection with the effects for senators
in those same states who were not on the ballot. More precisely, respondents in states with female Senate candidates or with swing Democrats
on the ballot should be more informed of their incumbent's vote than
they are about senators who were not up for reelection. Moreover, these
environmental cues should have been especially pronounced for those
respondents most engaged by the political campaign—the voters. For
this reason, the following results will focus only on respondents who reported voting in the 1992 Senate elections.

Logistic regression analyses are used to uncover these results (see appendix table 3B). As with the previous tables, these results are converted
into predicted probabilities to simplify interpretation. Table 3.5 presents
the probabilities for senators facing reelection in 1992 and for senators
in those same states who were not on the ballot. A number of important
findings emerge from this table. First, black voters in states with swing
Democrats on the ballot were significantly more likely than their white
counterparts to identify accurately their senators' vote on the Thomas
nomination. The difference across racial groups was about .29 for these

Table 3.5

Predicted Probability of Identifying Vote on Thomas Confirmation for Senators with Reelection Campaigns (Voters Only)

	Not Facing Reelection	Facing Reelection
Gender		
Women	.49	.37
Men	.61	.51
Race		
Blacks	.50	.36
Whites	.49	.37
Ideology and gender		
Liberal women	.66	.51
Liberal men	.45	.38
Conservative women	.46	.24
Conservative men	.72	.59
Political context		
Blacks in swing states	.55	.63
Whites in swing states	.47	.34
Female candidate	.52	.66
No female candidate	.49	.37
Electoral competition: high	.50	.46
Electoral competition: low	.49	.33

Source: 1988–1992 Senate Election Study.
Note: Probabilities are based on logistic regression analyses presented in table 3B.

senators. However, the racial gap is considerably smaller for the senators not up for reelection in these same states.

The effects of female Senate candidates are also significantly positive for senators facing reelection but indistinguishable from zero for senators not on the ballot. The probability that voters identified this vote correctly for senators facing reelection was about .66 in states with female candidates. The corresponding probability was about .37 for senators not facing reelection in these same states. Finally, respondents were also more informed about the vote of incumbents who faced strong challengers (.46 versus .33). As expected, this variable had no effect on senators who were not up for reelection.

Conclusion

The principal question this chapter sought to answer was whether perceptions of issue salience and external political factors increased levels of political information. The results indicate that they are important both separately and interactively. For example, conservative men, and to a lesser extent liberal women, were significantly more knowledgeable of their senators' vote on the Thomas nomination than were relevant comparison groups. Of course, it should be noted that respondents had a 50–50 chance of accurately guessing their senators' position on this vote. Although this may bias estimates of how many citizens actually possessed this information, it should not affect the results of this chapter. After all, there is no reason to believe that the issue publics focused on in this chapter were better guessers than other respondents. Indeed, if this were the case, then these respondents should have also been more knowledgeable about politics on issues in which they were not particularly interested. This was not the case.

Contextual factors were also associated with knowledge of the Thomas vote. Specifically, the presence of female Senate candidates was found to enhance accuracy rates on the Thomas vote for all respondents. On matters where the gender of the candidates was less important (e.g., the Gulf War vote), this variable had no effect. Similarly, the interaction of salience and political context also affected accuracy rates, although not always in the manner hypothesized. I expected that issue publics with special interest in the Thomas vote would be even more accurate in states represented by swing Democrats. This turned out to be true, however, only for African Americans. Still, these effects were considerable, especially for senators facing reelection. For these senators, blacks not only closed the traditional racial gap in political information but also far surpassed comparable whites.

Why has other research in this area uncovered less powerful and consistent evidence of selective attentiveness? Undoubtedly, part of the answer is that researchers have not always looked in the right places. While demographic characteristics are an appropriate proxy for issue salience, researchers need to be mindful that sometimes these characteristics can lead to less rather than more political attentiveness. Failure to take this complication into account can lead to an underestimation of salience effects. Thus, researchers operating under the assumption that most conservatives were concerned about the outcome of the Thomas vote would have found little evidence of selective attentiveness.

Another reason why some previous work has found limited support for the issue salience hypothesis is that insufficient attention has been paid to the political context. As the results of this chapter demonstrate, attentiveness to political matters can at times be enhanced by factors in the local political environment. Bobo and Gilliam (1990) have already shown that this can occur when the racial background of the mayor suggests accessibility to local residents. This chapter shows that even more subtle differences in the political environment can also increase information levels.

With regard to the debate between the generalist and the specialist models of political information processing, this chapter provides only a limited resolution. Both models account for some of the variation in respondents' knowledge of their senators' vote on the Thomas nomination. The generalist model, however, works much better for men than for women. Among men, the effects of the general measure of political knowledge are usually about twice the size of those of the salience measures. The one exception to this rule was the interaction of race and context. The size of these effects was essentially comparable to the size of the effects of general political knowledge. Also, among women, the generalist and specialists models led to roughly equivalent results.

Finally, identifying how much various groups knew about the position of their senators on the Thomas nomination helps to explain why Thomas succeeded in spite of the controversy sparked by his hearings. This chapter confirms that senators were right to be concerned with how their constituents might react. The constituents whom senators feared would be especially attentive were indeed more informed than others were. In the end, Thomas was successful because the issue publics most concerned with the vote were also not randomly distributed across the nation. The two groups most predisposed to support Thomas—blacks and conservative men—represented a potent, although unusual, coalition. They were also disproportionately concentrated in the states represented by swing Democrats.

The successful confirmation vote of Clarence Thomas to the U.S. Supreme Court was broadly responsive in the sense that most voters favored the nomination. The Senate vote was also more narrowly responsive as well because, according to media reports, many senators paid special attention to the concerns of voters with the most intense opinions on this issue. In spite of the consistent finding that information levels are typically low, legislators likely feared that if they voted "incorrectly," interested voters would learn of this and exact retribution at the ballot box. At a minimum, the results of this chapter suggest that this concern was a reasonable one.

Appendix to Chapter 3

Notes on Variables Used in Analyses

THE main dependent variable in this chapter is the respondents' ability to recall accurately how their senators voted on the confirmation of Clarence Thomas to the Supreme Court. When analyzing results from the full sample, this variable has three possible values—0, 0.5, and 1. Respondents coded as 1 accurately identified both of their senators' votes, whereas a score of 0.5 represents accurate knowledge of only one senator's vote, and 0 represents incorrect responses for both senators or an inability to provide an answer. Some additional analysis was also done on the Persian Gulf War vote (also coded 0–1). The point of examining this vote was to provide a baseline for comparison with the Thomas model.

The relevant individual-level variables are race (black or white respondents only), gender, and ideology. Ideology is measured in two ways. First and most broadly, ideology is measured with the standard 7-point ideological scale. This scale was recoded so that higher values represented a more liberal political orientation. The second measure of ideology is a respondent's position on the abortion question. This variable ranges from 1 to 3, with higher values indicating more support for abortion rights.

The contextual or environmental measures of selective attentiveness are the presence of a reelection campaign in the state, the relative competitiveness of this campaign, the presence of female candidates in the reelection campaign, and residence in a state represented by a swing Democrat.[23] Competitiveness is measured with *Congressional Quarterly's* assessment of the incumbent's electoral prospects and ranges from 0 to 4, with higher values indicating greater competitiveness.

Given my expectation that some group members should be more informed of their senators' vote than others should, these analyses also included a number of interaction terms. These include interactions for race by residence in a state with a swing Democrat, gender by ideology, and gender by abortion attitude. The models in tables 3A and 3B also include a number of standard control variables. These variables include respondents' level of political information, education, age, length of residence in the state, reported media usage, level of interest in campaigns, support or opposition to the Thomas nomination, and partisan and ideological strength. Separate analyses by gender showed that the informa-tion and ideological strength variables performed differently for men and women. For this reason, these variables were interacted with gender in the analyses described in this chapter.

Table 3A

Ordered Logistic Regression Models Predicting Knowledge of Senators' Vote on Confirmation of Clarence Thomas to U.S. Supreme Court and Gulf War Use of Force Resolution

Independent Variables	Thomas Vote		Gulf War	
	Logit	Standard Error	Logit	Standard Error
Political information (0–1)	1.47***	(0.27)	1.34***	(0.27)
Media use[a] (0–7)	0.04*	(0.02)	0.06***	(0.02)
Education (1–5)	0.12***	(0.03)	0.13***	(0.03)
Party strength[b] (0–3)	0.10**	(0.04)	0.15***	(0.04)
Campaign interest (1–3)	0.10	(0.07)	0.22***	(0.07)
Age (17–97)	−0.01***	(0.00)	−0.01***	(0.00)
Years in state (0–89)	0.01***	(0.00)	0.01***	(0.00)
Abortion attitudes (1–3)	0.00	(0.10)	0.05	(0.10)
Thomas/War[c] (0–1)	0.93***	(0.12)	0.61***	(0.11)
Ideology (1–7)	−0.08*	(0.05)	−0.05	(0.05)
Ideological strength[b] (0–3)	0.05	(0.06)	−0.01	(0.06)
Female (0–1)	−1.04**	(0.38)	−1.07*	(0.38)
Black (0–1)	−0.12	(0.20)	−0.31	(0.20)
Swing Democrat (0–1)	0.07	(0.12)	0.17	(0.12)
Female candidate (0–1)	0.65***	(0.12)	0.01	(0.13)
Election in state (0–1)	−0.50***	(0.16)	−0.04	(0.16)
Competitive election (0–4)	0.12*	(0.05)	−0.02	(0.06)
Interaction variables				
Black × Swing Democrat (0–1)	0.69**	(0.31)	0.36	(0.31)
Female × Ideology (0–7)	0.15**	(0.07)	0.08	(0.07)
Female × Ideology strength (0–3)	0.14*	(0.08)	0.22**	(0.08)
Female × Abortion attitude (0–3)	0.16	(0.13)	0.16	(0.13)
Female × Information (0–1)	−0.80*	(0.37)	−0.91**	(0.37)
Log likelihood	−2401.81		−2319.79	
Chi-square	342.84		343.76	
N	2,354		2,311	

Source: 1988–1992 Senate Election Study.

[a] This variable is a combination of two questions measuring how many days in the past week the respondent watched news programs on TV or read a daily newspaper. The variables were combined and divided by two.

[b] These variables measure the strength of the respondent's partisan or ideological attachment. Higher values indicate a stronger attachment to either the Republican or Democratic party, or conservative or liberal ideology.

[c] Respondents who took no position on the Gulf War vote or the Thomas vote were coded as 0, and respondents who either supported or opposed the action were coded as 1. In the Gulf War model only the Gulf War attitude question was included whereas in the Thomas model only the Thomas attitude question was included.

* $p \leq .05$; ** $p \leq .01$; *** $p \leq .001$ for one-tailed test, except constant.

Table 3B

Logistic Regression Models Predicting Knowledge of Senators' Vote on Confirmation of Clarence Thomas to U.S. Supreme Court

Independent Variables	Senator Not Facing Reelection		Senator Facing Reelection	
	Logit	Standard Error	Logit	Standard Error
Intercept	−0.99†	(0.71)	−1.70**	(.73)
Political information	2.01***	(0.54)	2.16***	(0.56)
Media use	−0.01	(0.04)	0.01	(0.04)
Education	0.12*	(0.06)	0.12*	(0.06)
Party strength	0.03	(0.08)	0.13*	(0.08)
Campaign interest	0.02	(0.13)	−0.15	(0.14)
Age	−0.00	(0.00)	−0.01†	(0.01)
Years in state	−0.00	(0.00)	0.01*	(0.00)
Abortion attitudes	−0.33*	(0.18)	0.02	(0.19)
Supported *or* opposed Thomas	1.08***	(0.23)	0.84***	(0.23)
Ideology	−0.08	(0.09)	−0.15*	(0.09)
Ideological strength	−0.04	(0.12)	−0.06	(0.13)
Female	−1.53*	(0.73)	−1.63**	(0.75)
Black	0.05	(0.33)	−0.06	(0.34)
Swing Democrat	−0.07	(0.20)	−0.14	(0.21)
Female candidate	0.10	(0.16)	1.18***	(0.17)
Competitive election	0.01	(0.08)	0.19**	(0.08)
Interaction variables				
Black × Swing Democrat	0.26	(0.53)	1.27**	(0.56)
Female × Ideology	0.24*	(0.12)	0.17†	(0.12)
Female × Ideological strength	0.19	(0.16)	0.04	(0.16)
Female × Abortion attitude	0.25	(0.24)	0.50*	(0.25)
Female × Information	−1.23*	(0.73)	−1.33*	(0.75)
% predicted correctly	60.74		65.24	
Chi-square	95.59		149.37	
−2 log likelihood	1136.57		1082.60	
N	889		889	

Source: 1988–1992 Senate Election Study.

Note: Table includes results for Senate election voters only.

† p ≤ .10; * p ≤ .05; ** p ≤ .01; *** p ≤ .001 for one-tailed test, except for constant.

Four

Perceptions of Issue Importance and Campaign Attentiveness

THE RESULTS from the previous chapter showed that citizens more concerned about a particular issue are also more attentive to their senators' vote on that issue, especially when environmental cues promote such attentiveness. This chapter moves beyond an emphasis on individual votes and instead focuses on more general attentiveness to campaign issue content. Specifically, this chapter addresses two related questions: Which citizens are most attentive to campaign information, and under what circumstances do they become especially informed?

As with the previous chapter, this chapter relies on the 1988–1992 Senate Election Study survey to answer the main questions. In addition to the survey data, I also rely upon a campaign content analysis of my own design. This content analysis of the Senate campaigns, described more fully below, differs from the one in chapter 2 in that it identifies the major policy issues raised in each of the campaigns *as well as an assessment of their prominence.* Taken together, the survey and campaign content data allow for the rare opportunity to assess how the electoral environment affects individual levels of attentiveness.

The Effects of the Political Environment on Information Levels

Do information levels in the mass public increase during the campaign season? Public opinion specialists are not in agreement on this question. Some argue that information levels are not only generally low among the mass public, but that they do not, as a rule, rise when candidates wage more issue-laden campaigns (Bennett 1995; Converse 1975; Margolis 1977; Smith 1989). Moreover, most voters appear unable to identify which issues are raised in local Senate campaigns (Dalager 1996). Dalager found that only about one-third of voters were able to name correctly at least one campaign issue from the 1988 Senate campaigns. Approximately 40 percent of voters were unable to identify any issue, and just slightly more than half of those that did so were accurate. This may result from inherent deficiencies in the mass public (Knight 1990; Smith

1989), the strategic decision of the candidates to avoid specific policy positions (Page 1978), or the tendency of the mass media to focus more on so-called horse-race themes rather than substantive policy questions (Patterson 1994; Patterson and McClure 1976).

Some scholars argue that voters did become more informed about the issue positions of the two parties during the turbulent 1960s (relative to the 1950s) when the parties policy differences became more distinctive (Nie, Verba, and Petrocik 1976; Pomper 1972; Repass 1971). As it turns out, however, these findings were based almost entirely on changes in the questionnaire format utilized by the National Election Studies (Sullivan, Piereson, and Marcus 1979). Additionally, Carmines and Stimson (1980) argue that any true increase in the clarity of the parties' policy positions derived mostly from the "easy issue" of race.[1] They find that, in spite of the turmoil associated with protests of the Vietnam War, this "hard issue" did not provoke more information about the parties' respective positions.

In contrast to this research, many other scholars argue that citizens do become more informed when political information becomes more pervasive—as during high-profile election periods. For example, the early Columbia scholars as well as more recent work confirm that campaigns reduce uncertainty and provide voters with the necessary information ultimately to cast a ballot consistent with their underlying predispositions (Alvarez 1997; Berelson, Lazarsfeld, and McPhee 1954; Gelman and King 1993; Petrocik 1996; Zaller 1992). This holds true at the presidential level as well at lower levels of government. Thus, scholars have shown that exposure to media messages during Senate campaigns increases information about the candidates (Goldenberg and Traugott 1987; West 1994). Similarly, when policy matters are emphasized in Senate campaigns, voters become more certain of their position on the issues (Franklin 1991).

If campaigns do have the effect of increasing voter information levels, then which voters are most susceptible? Dalager (1996) finds, not surprisingly, that individual characteristics such as education and political interest are the best predictors of campaign learning. Luskin (1990), however, places less faith in education per se and more in political interest. Finally, Zaller (1992) argues that citizens who are routinely attentive to political matters are most likely to be exposed to campaign messages. In a similar vein, Price and Zaller (1993) also find that individuals with high levels of general news consumption are most likely to learn about any particular news story. Alternatively, these authors found little support for the issue publics' perspective.

This chapter adopts a different point of view. As indicated in figure 1.1, I believe that individuals with a particular interest in an issue will be more likely than others to recognize when those issues are prominently

featured in campaigns. As it turns out, research on agenda setting provides some support for this proposition. Agenda setting occurs when the
issues covered by the media also become more salient for the viewing
audience. Using National Election Study survey data and a content analysis of their own design, Erbring, Goldenberg, and Miller (1980) show
that agenda setting more powerfully affects the issue priorities of citizens
who are already interested in the topic. For example, they report that
individuals living in union households are more likely than other citizens
to identify unemployment or the recession as important issues if their
local media source has recently devoted considerable attention to the
issue. Similar results are uncovered for the issue of race relations among
African Americans, and among women and the issue of crime. Iyengar
and Kinder (1987) report essentially the same results using experimental
data.

This work is significant because it provides compelling evidence that
the impact of media messages is sometimes contingent on perceptions
of issue importance. This chapter extends previous work in this area by
arguing that the interaction of issue importance and contextual factors
not only affects citizens' issue priorities, but also the amount of factual
information they will absorb. Specifically, this chapter will show that not
all citizens take away the same information from election campaigns.
Those with a prior interest in a topic will be far more likely than other
citizens to recognize when "their" issue is raised in the campaign.

Measuring Issue Importance

As in chapter 3, perceptions of issue importance are gauged indirectly
by relying on the available demographic and attitudinal information contained in the SES survey.[2] However, this chapter relies on a different set
of issue publics from those identified in the previous chapter. My decision on which issue publics to select was based largely on how frequently
various issues were raised in the 1988–1992 Senate campaigns (see appendix to this chapter). As it turns out, those issues most frequently discussed, which also have an obvious relationship to a specific set of interests, are labor issues, defense issues, and abortion.[3]

Following the lead of Erbring, Goldenberg, and Miller (1980), I sur-
mised that union members and citizens living in union households
would be most interested in labor issues. In the case of defense issues,
gender and partisanship were identified as indicators of perceived importance. One of the most enduring gender differences in public opinion involves the use of violence. Women are consistently less approving
of policies involving violence, both domestically and internationally, than

are men (Page and Shapiro 1992; Shapiro and Mahajan 1986; Smith 1984). Additionally, policies related to national defense represent one of the most important issues that define the two major political parties (Petrocik 1996). Consequently, and similar to my argument in chapter 3, I hypothesize that citizens most likely to respond viscerally to defense issues are Republican men and Democratic women. These two groups are likely to be less conflicted on this issue and consequently most attentive, albeit for different reasons, when it is raised in campaigns.

Although studies have found that women and men show few differences in their attitudes concerning abortion, women are somewhat more likely to adopt "extreme" positions on both sides of the issue (Luker 1984; Yeric and Todd 1996). Also, the biggest supporters of abortion rights tend to be upper-status women (Luker 1984). Among pro-choice individuals, previous research has also found that women regard the issue of abortion as more important than do men (Scott and Schuman 1988). Similarly, a number of studies have shown that the strongest opponents of abortion are religious conservatives (Cook, Jelen, and Wilcox 1992; Luker 1984; Yeric and Todd 1996). For these reasons, I conclude that the abortion issue will be perceived as more important to women (especially upper-status women) and religious conservatives. As a result, these groups should be more likely than others to recognize when this issue is raised in campaigns.[4]

Measuring Campaign Content

This chapter relies heavily upon a content analysis of the 1988–1992 Senate campaign cycle. It was specifically designed to complement the 1988–1992 Senate Election Study that is the source of all survey results in this and the subsequent chapter. There are two characteristics of this content analysis that deserve mention here. First, this chapter only examines races where incumbent senators are facing reelection. This decision was made because the primary focus of this book is on the ability of citizens to acquire information on (and ultimately hold accountable) their representatives *while in office*. Second, this content analysis was expressly designed to capture both the discussion of various issues in the campaign and their level of prominence.

Three coders were selected to summarize the campaign themes after reading several journalistic accounts of the each contest.[5] These sources are the *Congressional Quarterly's Special Report on the Elections*, various editions of *Politics in America*, and the *Almanac of American Politics*. These sources were selected because they gave a broad overview of the incumbents' previous legislative history and their most recent campaign.

Coders were instructed to first "identify the main *political* issues raised in each of the Senate campaigns involving an incumbent from 1988 to 1992. Candidate-oriented themes such as the age or health of a candidate, attacks on their ethics or character, etc., are not the subject of this project." Second, they were instructed to "judge the prominence of each issue from the point of view of a typical voter who happened to be interested in this issue." The prominence of an issue was assessed, roughly, as the probability that an interested voter would learn of the campaign discussion involving the issue and ranged from 0 to 100 (see appendix to this chapter for complete instructions).

The first two coders examined the appropriate sources and provided their best judgment as to what issues were raised and how prominently they were discussed. A third coder was used to reconcile disagreements between the first two over whether or not an issue was raised. In some cases, the third coder also examined campaigns where the first two coders disagreed not with each other but with my own prior coding. The decisions of this third coder were then substituted for the results of the coder with whom she disagreed, and the salience level was averaged across the two scores.

Issue Publics and Campaign Learning

The study design adopted to test the hypothesis that salience will enhance campaign learning is a simple one. The model includes the two variables described above (i.e., the salience level of a given issue, and membership in the relevant issue public) and their interaction. Additionally, the models control for partisan strength, ideological strength, income, media consumption habits, campaign interest, campaign competitiveness, and challenger spending. The explanatory, or dependent, variable is whether respondents accurately identify the relevant issue debated in the campaign.[6] If perceptions of issue importance do influence attentiveness, then interested citizens should be most likely to accurately identify "their" issues.

Labor Issues and Union Membership

Before examining attentiveness to labor issues, let us explore in some detail which campaigns devoted the most attention to labor issues. Table 4A in the appendix to this chapter shows the campaigns where issues relevant to union members were raised and the average score of these issues on the issue prominence measure. It is striking how infrequently labor issues (trade, plant closings, jobs, etc.) were raised during this period. These issues were raised in only six contests in 1988 and three contests in 1992. They were totally absent in 1990. This underscores a point first made in chapter 1: voters are not often confronted with issue-laden campaigns.

It is also interesting that the campaigns where union issues arose are disproportionately represented by states with large numbers of union members. Of the nine states, all but North Dakota and New Mexico had either average or greater than average percentages of union respondents. Moreover, the percentage of union members in the three states where labor issues were most prominent is about 15 percent, whereas in the remaining states this percentage is only 8 percent.[7] Thus, it is possible that union issues were prominently raised in these particular states because there organized labor still commands enough strength to force its issues onto the political agenda.

A closer examination of the three campaigns bears this out. In the 1988 Ohio campaign, veteran Democratic Senator Howard Metzenbaum faced challenger George Voinovich. Metzenbaum, described in the *Almanac of American Politics* as "probably the strongest backer of organized labor," campaigned on a number of themes, including his leadership role on the highly popular Plant Closing Notification Bill (for description, see chapter 2). This legislation was the chief priority of organized labor in the one-hundredth Congress.

In the 1992 Oregon contest, incumbent Republican Senator Robert Packwood faced a touch challenger in Democratic representative Les Aucoin. Aucoin came out early in opposition to the proposed North Atlantic Free Trade Agreement and was criticized for this position by Packwood. In the 1988 Michigan race, incumbent Democratic Senator Donald W. Riegle ran for reelection largely through a number of television ads, including one featuring New Jersey Senator Bill Bradley likening Riegle's efforts on recent trade legislation to that of a championship athletic leader. This trade bill "provide[d] for government retaliation against unfair marketing practices by foreign competitors and authorize[d] $1 billion for retraining workers who lose jobs because of imports."[8]

Figure 4.1 shows how identification rates vary as labor issues become increasingly visible. This figure is based on probabilities derived from a logistic regression model, which also includes standard demographic controls (see table 4D in the appendix to this chapter). The figure presents results for union members, respondents who live in union households but are not union members, and nonunion members. As hypothesized, the best predictor of accurately identifying whether or not labor issues are present in the campaign is membership in a labor union.[9] When labor issues are virtually absent from the campaign, the probability is only about .12 that union members will identify these issues as one of the most talked-about issues in the election. However, when labor issues become more prominent, this probability approaches .50. The sharpest

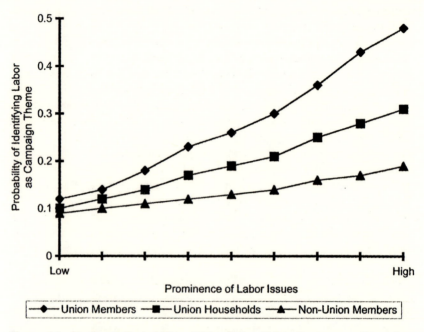

Figure 4.1. Predicted Probability of Identifying Labor Issues as a Campaign Theme for Union Members, Respondents in Union Households, and Other Respondents. Probabilities are based on logistic regression analyses in table 4D. (Source: 1988–1992 Senate Election Study)

rise in attentiveness seems to come after prominence levels exceed the .50 mark. Respondents who live in union households but are not themselves union members are also attentive to labor issues, although not to the same degree as union members. They also become most alert when labor issues are at least moderately prominent. Finally, respondents with no connection to unions are the least attentive to union-related issues. Even when these issues are at the peak of their prominence, the probability that non-union-affiliated citizens will notice is just shy of .20.

Defense Issues and Gender and Partisanship

Of the three issues focused on in this chapter, defense is by far the most likely to emerge as a campaign theme. Defense-related issues were raised in twenty-four of the eighty-six Senate races involving an incumbent between 1988 and 1992. By contrast, labor issues and abortion were raised in only nine and fourteen campaigns, respectively. Issues of defense are, of course, more likely to appeal to a larger audience than the other two topics. Another reason for the relative prominence of defense issues was undoubtedly the Gulf War crisis of 1990–1991.

Virtually all of the campaigns where defense issues were most prominently raised involved direct or indirect reference to the Gulf War. For example, the two campaigns where defense issues received the most attention were in Rhode Island in 1990 and Georgia in 1992. The Rhode Island race involved a contest between the seventy-one-year-old incumbent Democratic Senator Claiborne Pell and a much younger challenger, Claudine Schneider. Schneider's primary theme was that the incumbent's advanced age undermined his effectiveness. To respond to the charge that he was out of touch, Pell scheduled a highly publicized visit to the troops stationed in the Middle East (apparently to demonstrate his support). In the Georgia campaign, incumbent Democratic Senator Wyche Fowler faced a tough challenge from Paul Coverdell. Coverdell attacked the incumbent on a number of fronts, including his vote in opposition to the use of force in the Gulf War. Other campaigns that also featured prominent references to the Gulf War include the 1990 Michigan race (where the Republican challenger implied that the incumbent did not fully support the troops because he opposed appropriations for various weapons projects) and the 1992 North Carolina race (where the Republican challenger ran television ads criticizing the incumbent for voting against the use-of-force resolution).

Which voters were most likely to hear about this issue when it was raised? My expectation was that (antidefense) Democratic women and (prodefense) Republican men would be most attentive to this issue.[10] This hypothesis was only partially confirmed. As it turns out, neither Republican men nor Democratic men were especially sensitive to defense issues (see table 4E in the appendix to this chapter). Among women, the results were more in keeping with expectations. Women showed a moderate tendency to identify defense issues as prominent as they received greater attention in the campaign. Moreover, this effect occurred only among Democratic women who opposed greater spending on defense, as shown in figure 4.2. The probability of identifying defense issues as a campaign theme rose from essentially zero when the issue was not mentioned to almost .25 when the issue reached its maximum level of salience. Among Republican women who supported greater spending on defense, the equivalent effect was essentially flat.

Religion, Gender, Status, and the Abortion Controversy

As indicated above, the issue of abortion was raised in fourteen of the eighty-six Senate races studied in this chapter. The issue was raised in only two campaigns in 1988, but it was mentioned in six in both 1990

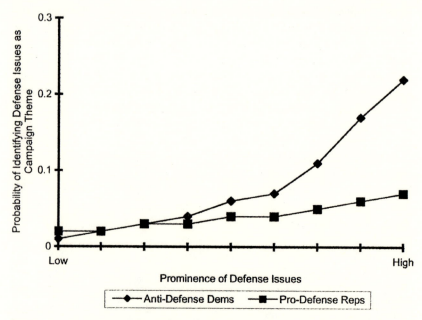

Figure 4.2. Predicted Probability of Identifying Defense Issues as a Campaign Theme for Anti-Defense-Spending Democrats and Pro-Defense-Spending Republicans (Women Only). Probabilities are based on logistic regression analyses in table 4E. (Source: 1988–1992 Senate Election Study)

and 1992. The issue did not arise as frequently as some might suspect because it is not in the short-term interest of either party to publicize it. Democrats and especially Republicans are divided on this question, and generally it is more strategic for the two parties simply to avoid the issue whenever possible. Typically, politicians would rather avoid divisive issues and instead focus on broadly popular issues, such as the environment, tax cuts, or opposition to crime. Abortion is one of the most contentious issues on the national scene. Still, the pro-life and pro-choice forces are sufficiently organized that they can sometimes force the issue onto the agenda even when party elites would have it otherwise.

An examination of the campaigns where abortion was most prominently discussed illustrates that the issue is frequently raised only when demanded by activists or when a candidate sees a clear advantage. In 1990 abortion was most heavily debated in North Carolina, Oregon, and, to a lesser extent, Iowa. In 1992, campaigns in Ohio and North Carolina devoted considerable attention to the issue. In the 1990 North Carolina campaign, Republican incumbent Senator Jesse Helms charged in television ads that his opponent, Democrat Harvey Gantt, supported abortion in the final weeks of pregnancy and for purposes of sex selection (positions even many pro-choice voters would find objectionable). Abortion rights groups, on the other hand, ran ads attacking Helms's uncompromising pro-life stance. Unlike most other senators, Helms feels comfortable staking out positions on divisive issues in part because of his background as an editorialist for a local television station. It also worth noting that a pro-life position on abortion is not terribly risky in a state where, according to the SES, almost half (43%) of the residents are fundamentalist Protestants.

Oregon almost represents a mirror image of North Carolina. In 1990 conservative activists managed to place two referendums on the November ballot concerning abortion. One required parental consent for minors seeking an abortion, while the other banned the procedure outright. The former lost on a close 52–48 percent vote while the ban went down by an overwhelming 68–32 percent. In large part because of the publicity surrounding the abortion issue, Democratic challenger Harry Lonsdale, along with the National Abortion Rights Action League and the National Organization of Women, criticized incumbent Senator Mark Hatfield for his pro-life stance.

In the 1990 Iowa contest, incumbent Democratic Senator Tom Harkin was in a race with challenger Tom Tauke deemed too close to call by the *Congressional Quarterly.* Most interesting for our purposes, however, was that NARAL and other pro-choice groups were extremely visible in this campaign. These groups spent considerable effort mobilizing support for the incumbent. The 1992 Ohio campaign also involved a close race between long-time Democratic incumbent Senator John Glenn and Republican Lt. Governor Mike Dewine. Glenn, still suffering from his ties to the savings and loan scandal, was considered the most vulnerable senator in 1992 by the GOP and was targeted for defeat. Because of this, Glenn went on the attack early. One of his more consistent messages was that Dewine was opposed to abortion rights. Dewine, apparently stung by the charge, aired television ads featuring his wife and making the point that he respects differing views and the issue should not be politicized.

Finally, in the 1992 North Carolina campaign incumbent Democratic Senator Terry Sanford faced an ultimately successful challenge from Republican Lauch Faircloth. Although Faircloth was a Democrat as recently as 1984, he was backed by Jesse Helms's Congressional Club and consequently took conservative stands on all the major issues, including abortion. While Sanford ran ads criticizing Faircloth's "flip-flop" on abortion, in the end he simply ran a lackluster campaign (partly because of health problems). It is also interesting that he did not criticize Faircloth for being pro-life but merely for changing his position.

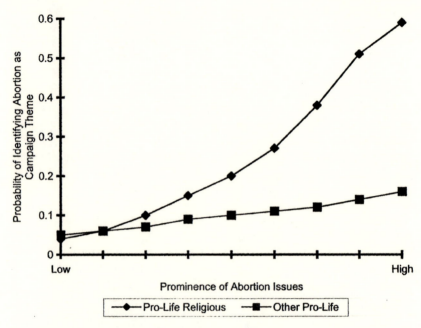

Figure 4.3. Predicted Probability of Identifying Abortion as a Campaign Theme for Pro-Life Protestant Fundamentalists and Catholics, and Other Pro-Life Respondents. Probabilities are based on logistic regression analyses in table 4F. (Source: 1988–1992 Senate Election Study)

In assessing the relationship between interest in abortion and campaign learning, we first examine results for Catholics and fundamentalist Protestants.[11] Unfortunately, the SES does not provide any other religious questions beyond self-identification so it is difficult to isolate those respondents who are most committed to religious conservatism. It would have been preferable, for example, if respondents were asked about the literal interpretation of the Bible, or how often they attend church, or how important religion is in their day-to-day living (Barker and Carman 1997). However, the SES does provide a question on abortion that I used to identify the most morally conservative Catholics and fundamentalists. Thus, for my purposes, the religious issue-public consists of self-identified white Catholics and Protestant fundamentalists who also indicate that they are unequivocally pro-life.

Figure 4.3 shows how accuracy rates for identification of abortion as a campaign theme vary for religious pro-life advocates and other respondents. As expected, both groups identify this theme more often as it becomes more prominent in the campaign, but the slope is over twice as large for pro-life Protestant fundamentalists and Catholics. When abortion is not a significant issue in the election campaign, almost no respon-

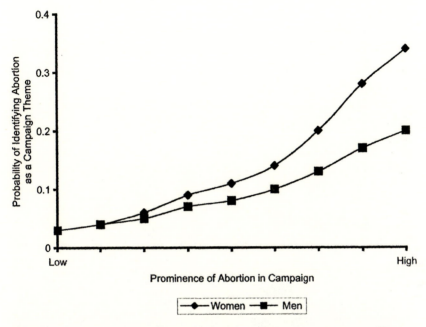

Figure 4.4. Predicted Probability of Identifying Abortion as a Campaign Theme for Women and Men. Probabilities are based on logistic regression analyses in table 4G. (Source: 1988–1992 Senate Election Study)

dents identified it as important. However, as this issue becomes more prominent, pro-life religious conservatives become especially attentive. When the issue reaches the maximum level of prominence, the probability that these respondents will correctly identify the issue is almost .60. In contrast, the probability that other pro-life respondents will recognize the issue, even when it is exceptionally prominent, never rises above .20.

Another group for whom the abortion issue should be especially important is women. This is particularly true for women with high socioeconomic backgrounds.[12] Before examining this latter group, however, let us first look into results for men and women more broadly. As shown in figure 4.4, all respondents are more likely to identify abortion as a campaign theme when it is in fact more prominent in the election. However, the effects are strongest for women, particularly after prominence levels rise above .50. Among women, the predicted probability of identifying abortion as a major campaign theme rises from about .03, when the issue is not at all prominent, to about .35, when it is extremely visible. For men, the probabilities only increase from .03 to .20.

The gender differences on attentiveness to the abortion issue grow even larger when we shift our focus to upper-middle-class respondents. These results are presented in figure 4.5. Here we see that high-status

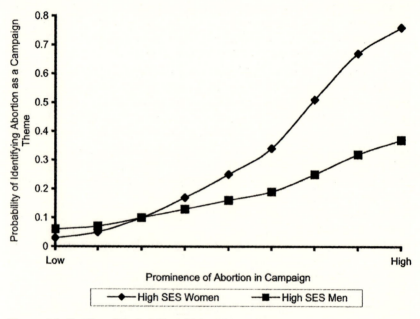

Figure 4.5. Predicted Probability of Identifying Abortion as a Campaign Theme for High SES Women and High SES Men. Probabilities are based on logistic regression analyses in table 4G. (Source: 1988–1992 Senate Election Study)

women are considerably more informed on this issue than their male counterparts. These gender differences are quite stark, with women becoming informed at rates of over two times those of comparable men as abortion increases in salience. For example, when the prominence of abortion issues is at its highest level, the probability that high-status women will recognize the presence of this issue is .76. Alternatively, the probability of attentiveness for high-status men is less than half this figure at .37. As in all of the previous analyses, I also examined whether general interest in political campaigns, education, or high media consumption affected knowledge of this campaign theme. None of these variables, however, had a significant effect on the dependant variable.[13]

Conclusion

This chapter sought to show that issue publics, or citizens with particular interests in specific issues, showed higher levels of campaign-specific attentiveness when "their" issues were raised in an election. This hypothesis was explored across three different issues and several different groups.

In general, my expectations were confirmed. With the exception of Republican men and defense issues, all of the issue publics examined in this chapter were better able than the comparison group to identify relevant issues when they arose in Senate campaigns.

That the results would hold across a number of different issues suggests that perceptions of issue importance do significantly influence campaign learning. Although the findings were strongest on the "easy" issue of abortion, as the work of Carmines and Stimson (1980) would suggest (see also Adams 1997), the results were almost as strong on the presumably "harder" labor issues. Results were considerably weaker, although still in the right direction, for attentiveness to defense issues. In general, it seems that whatever the complexity of the issue, stronger levels of interest promote greater political attentiveness.

The relationship uncovered in this chapter between interest and information does not extend to more general levels of political interest. Only respondents with specific interest in a given issue were likely to notice when it became prominent in the campaign. Respondents who indicated high levels of general political interest (whether measured by education, interest in political campaigns, or frequent news consumption) were consistently less knowledgeable than members of the issue publics. This finding builds on the results in chapter 3 but runs counter to previous work on the learning capacity of issue publics (Delli Carpini and Keeter 1996; Price and Zaller 1993).[14]

As with chapter 3, these results demonstrate that politicians are wise to respond to their constituents' potential preferences. As political scientists have consistently demonstrated, most citizens are not attentive to political issues most of the time. However, if issues that they find important emerge on the political scene, for whatever reason, citizens can become quickly informed. In the next chapter, I examine whether this heightened attentiveness translates into a greater likelihood on the part of issue publics to reward their "friends" and punish their "enemies" at the ballot box.

*Appendix to Chapter 4*_____

Coder Instructions

Your overall task is to, FIRST, identify the main *political* issues raised in each of the eighty-six Senate campaigns involving an incumbent from 1988 to 1992. Candidate-oriented themes such as the age or health of a candidate, attacks on their ethics or character, etc., are not the subject of this project. SECOND, you are instructed to judge the prominence of each issue from the point of view of a typical voter who happened to be interested in this issue.

Your coding judgments should be based solely on summary descriptions of the campaign as provided to you from the *Almanac of American Politics, Congressional Quarterly's Politics in America*, and the *Congressional Quarterly Weekly Report's Special Election Year Issues*. Coders will assess the campaigns after reading all of the sources accounts. Also, it should be noted that while these sources overlap considerably, they deal with slightly different time frames. That is, the *Almanac of American Politics* and *Politics in America* are published *after* the elections and summarize the entire campaigns. *Congressional Quarterly's Special Election Year Issues* are typically published in mid to late October and thus only describe events up to that time.

To assist in identifying issues, coders will be given a list of likely issue themes (but you need not be confined to issues on the list). For each issue listed on the coding sheet, you will answer the following two questions:

1. Was this issue theme raised in the campaign?
2. [IF YES] Think about a voter who happened to be interested in this issue and was moderately attentive to the campaign. How likely would it be that such a voter would become aware of campaign discussion of this issue? [1%–100%]

In making these judgments, you should make use of all information in your sources, including (if available) the following: information about the overall intensity of the campaign; whether both candidates addressed the issue or only one; indications that the issue was raised often (i.e., was it one of the candidates core messages?); whether it became the subject of campaign advertising; whether the media gave it extensive discussion; whether it was the only issue in the campaign, one of few, or only one of many. You may take account of any special circumstances that you think are relevant. In some cases, the personal characteristics of the candidate(s) may increase the salience of the issue (e.g., an openly gay candidate who is attacked for favoring homosexuals in the military). In other cases, there may be a history of concern with the issue in the state (e.g., racial issues in the South, relations with Cuba in Florida, grazing fees in Wyoming, offshore oil drilling in California). In sum, your task is to determine which issues were raised in the various Senate campaigns, and the salience of each issue.

Coders were instructed to code up to thirteen different issues, including the environment, crime, and references to the balanced budget debate. However, only three broad set of issues were used in this book. This was largely because other issues with a clear association with particular groups were infrequently mentioned (e.g., race and social security). The issues emphasized in this chapter are described below.

1. **Abortion**—Take into account references to parental consent restrictions or waiting-period references. Also be aware of issues involving public funding of abortions. Sometimes "family planning" also involves the abortion issue.

2. **Defense/Foreign Policy**—Includes references to the Persian Gulf War. Might also include comments about a candidate's failure to serve in the military, with the implicit message being that they are soft on defense. This category also includes any references to American relations (NONTRADE) with foreign nations. Includes discussion of weapons systems.

3. **Plant Closing/Trade/NAFTA**—Specific references to the 1988 Plant Closing bill (requiring 60 days' notice before workers could be fired) opposed by the Reagan administration. This does NOT include any references to local plants. Comments on trade, including references to trade imbalance, import quotas, and exports particularly (but NOT only) when it is implied that Americans might lose jobs because of foreign trade. Finally, any references to the North American Free Trade Agreement that was designed to lower tariffs among the nations of Mexico, U.S., and Canada.

Table 4A
States Where Labor Issues Were Raised and the Average Level of Prominence

	Average Prominence Levels	
State	*1988*	*1992*
Delaware	42.5	—
Pennsylvania	40	—
Michigan	55	—
Ohio	50	—
North Dakota	30	—
New Mexico	40	—
Indiana	—	47.5
Missouri	—	45
Oregon	—	62.5

Table 4B
States Where Defense Issues Were Raised and the
Average Level of Prominence

	Average Prominence Levels		
State	*1988*	*1990*	*1992*
Connecticut	35	—	52.5
Maine	52.5	37.5	—
Massachusetts	—	55	—
Rhode Island	42.5	62.5	—
New Jersey	42.5	—	—
New York	—	—	52.5
Michigan	—	52.5	—
Wisconsin	—	—	30
Kansas	—	32.5	—
Minnesota	24.5	—	—
Missouri	26	—	—
Georgia	—	—	62.5
North Carolina	—	52.5	55
South Carolina	—	—	47.5
Texas	24.5	—	—
Kentucky	—	31	27.5
Montana	47.5	—	—
Wyoming	—	47.5	—
Hawaii	—	39	—

Table 4C

States Where the Abortion Issue Was Raised and the
Average Level of Prominence

	Average Prominence Levels		
State	1988	1990	1992
West Virginia	37.5	—	—
Utah	32.5	—	—
Iowa	—	60	—
North Carolina	—	87.5	60
Montana	—	35	—
Wyoming	—	27.5	—
Oregon	—	80	—
Alaska	—	40	20
Ohio	—	—	70
Missouri	—	—	40
Georgia	—	—	45
Oregon	—	—	40

Table 4D

Logistic Regression Model Predicting Effects of Residence in a Union
Household and Union Membership on Recognition of Labor-Related
Campaign Themes (1988 and 1992)

	Coefficients	Standard Error
Constant	−2.76***	(0.35)
Labor campaign prominence (0–1)	0.84**	(0.34)
Union relative or member (0–2)	0.18*	(0.10)
Union member × Labor prominence (0–2)	0.51[†]	(0.39)
% predicted correctly	86.91	
Chi-square	58.81***	
−2 log likelihood	1967.66	
N	2,621	

Source: 1988–1992 Senate Election Study.

Note: The model also controlled for media consumption, income, gender, partisan strength, ideological strength, race, campaign interest, campaign competitiveness, and challenger spending.

[†] $p \leq .10$; * $p \leq .05$; ** $p \leq .01$; *** $p \leq .001$ for one-tailed test, except constant.

Table 4E

Logistic Regression Model Predicting Effects of Partisanship and Attitudes on Defense Spending on Recognition of Defense-Related Campaign Themes (1988–1992)

	Men	*Women*
Constant	−4.89***	−6.95***
	(0.70)	(0.91)
Defense campaign prominence (0–1)	1.55	−0.00
	(1.75)	(1.99)
Party identification (1–7)	0.09	.03
	(0.08)	(0.09)
Defense attitudes (−1, 0, 1)	0.24	0.03
	(0.48)	(0.55)
Defense attitudes × Defense campaign prominence	0.29	−3.37†
	(1.98)	(2.32)
Party × Defense campaign prominence	−0.31	0.21
	(0.39)	(0.38)
Party × Defense attitudes	−0.03	0.04
	(0.10)	(0.12)
Party × Attitudes × Campaign prominence	−0.49	0.45
	(0.45)	(0.49)
% predicted correctly	96.96	97.98
Chi-square	36.62***	36.07***
−2 log likelihood	620.61	453.03
N	2,060	2,473

Source: 1988–1992 Senate Election Study.

Note: The model also controlled for partisan strength, ideological strength, income, media consumption, campaign interest, campaign competitiveness, and challenger spending.

† $p \leq .10$; * $p \leq .05$; ** $p \leq .01$; *** $p \leq .001$ for one-tailed test, except constant.

Table 4F

Logistic Regression Model Predicting Effects of Religion and Attitudes about Abortion on Recognition of Abortion as a Campaign Theme (1988–1992)

	Coefficients	Standard Error
Constant	−4.38***	(0.34)
Abortion campaign prominence (0–1)	2.51***	(0.31)
Pro-life on abortion (0, 1)	0.60**	(0.27)
Fundamentalist Protestant or Catholic (0, 1)	−0.12	(0.20)
Campaign prominence × fundamentalist	0.10	(0.50)
Campaign prominence × Pro-life	−1.33†	(0.94)
Pro-life × Fundamentalist or Catholic	−0.13	(0.43)
Campaign prominence × Pro-life × Fundamentalist or Catholic	2.17*	(1.25)
% predicted correctly	95.21	
Chi-square	147.67***	
−2 log likelihood	1785.12	
N	5,010	

Source: 1988–1992 Senate Election Study.

Note: The model also controlled for partisan strength, ideological strength, media consumption, gender, campaign interest, campaign competitiveness, and challenger spending.

† $p \leq .10$; * $p \leq .05$; ** $p \leq .01$; *** $p \leq .001$ for one-tailed test, except constant.

Table 4G

Logistic Regression Model Predicting Effects of Gender and Social Status on Recognition of Abortion as a Campaign Theme (1988–1992)

	Model 1	Model 2
Constant	–3.71***	–3.77***
	(.35)	(0.35)
Abortion campaign prominence (0–1)	2.13***	2.47***
	(0.37)	(0.25)
Female (0, 1)	0.02	0.19†
	(0.17)	(0.15)
High-social-status men (0, 1)	—	0.15
		(0.34)
High-social-status women (0, 1)	—	–0.66
		(0.55)
Campaign prominence × Female	0.67†	—
	(0.45)	
Campaign prominence × High-status men	—	–0.25
		(0.95)
Campaign prominence × High-status women	—	2.08*
		(1.14)
% predicted correctly	95.17	95.15
Chi-square	155.89***	157.38***
–2 log likelihood	1775.13	1773.64
N	4,992	4,992

Source: 1988–1992 Senate Election Study.

Note: See text for definition of social status. The models also controlled for partisan strength, ideological strength, media consumption, campaign interest, age, campaign competitiveness, and challenger spending.

† $p \leq .10$; * $p \leq .05$; ** $p \leq .01$; *** $p \leq .001$ for one-tailed test.

Five

Priming Issues during Senate Campaigns

THE EARLY literature on public opinion concluded that public policy issues rarely affect citizens' vote choice. Instead, scholars argued that social-psychological attitudes learned in childhood, such as party identification or membership in social groups, more strongly influence vote decisions (Campbell et al. 1960; Converse 1964; Lazarsfeld, Berelson, and Gaudet 1944). More recent work in this literature finds that these conclusions were somewhat overstated (Aldrich, Sullivan, and Borgida 1989; Fiorina 1981; Kinder and Kiewiet 1981; Rabinowitz and MacDonald 1989). Clearly, issues do affect the vote decision. What remains unclear in the literature, however, is the *circumstances* under which issue voting will occur.

In this chapter, I again focus on citizens especially concerned about labor issues, defense issues, and the abortion controversy. These issues are selected in part for reasons outlined in chapter 4 but also because of their diversity. These policies can be characterized as both "easy" and "hard" as well as foreign and domestic issues. Some scholars argue that whenever issue voting does emerge in the electorate, it typically involves so-called easy, or less complex, issues such as race or abortion (Adams 1997; Carmines and Stimson 1980). Including issues of both types will allow me to determine if issue voting is less prevalent on more difficult issues.

This chapter addresses two questions. First, are citizens who are concerned about a specific set of issues also more likely than others to consider their incumbent's performance on those issues at election time? Second, is this more likely to occur when issues of concern are prominently raised in election campaigns? A related question, also pursued in this chapter, is whether the relationship between issue salience and vote choice is stronger on less complicated issues.

There have been few examinations of this kind in the literature on issue voting. Most previous work has examined the impact of perceptions of issue prominence on the vote choice, or the effects of the political environment, or priming, on candidate evaluations, but rarely are both factors considered simultaneously. Those studies that do take up both questions typically concentrate on only a single election. As a result, we know little about how issue salience and campaign context interact *across* campaign settings. Part of the reason for this is that the priming literature has heretofore focused almost exclusively on presidential evaluations. Given the prominence of this office to the American political system, this emphasis is understandable. Still, there are certain benefits to focusing on Senate elections. For one thing, since roughly one-third of senators are up for reelection every two years, Senate elections occur far more frequently than do presidential elections. Thus, more opportunities are available to study the effects of particular issue agendas. Additionally, efforts to measure the campaign environment are far more manageable at the state, rather than the national, level. Indeed, this is part of the reason that the earliest campaign studies focused on the local level (Lazarsfeld, Berelson, and Gaudet 1944). For these reasons, I believe that an emphasis on Senate elections (and later, in chapters 6 and 7, gubernatorial elections) provides a good opportunity to study the relationships among issue prominence, issue salience, and the vote decision.

Issues, Issue Voting, and the Campaign Environment

For many years, the conventional wisdom in the study of voting and elections was that voters largely relied on their partisan considerations. We now know that retrospective judgments about the economy and, perhaps less prominently, more prospective judgments on a range of topics can also affect the vote choice (see, for example, Abramowitz 1995; Aldrich, Sullivan, and Borgida 1989; Cook, Jelen, and Wilcox 1994; Fiorina 1981; Kinder and Kiewiet 1981; Rabinowitz and MacDonald 1989). However, the literature is still unclear about what factors lead to greater amounts of issue voting.

The authors of *The American Voter* were among the earliest group of scholars to address this question (Campbell et al. 1960). They indicated that three conditions were necessary in order for citizens to engage in issue voting. The first was that the voter must be aware of the existence of the issue. Second, the voter must regard the issue as at least minimally important. Finally, the voter must believe that one party (or candidate) represents his or her position better than the other party (or candidate). Campbell and his colleagues found that only about 20–35 percent of citizens in the late 1950s and early 1960s were able to meet all three criteria.

Somewhat later, V. O. Key offered an additional condition. He argued that the candidates must also clearly enunciate their policy differences. In other words, part of the reason that issue voting happened so infrequently was that the candidates often avoided issue-laden campaigns. When issues were emphasized, Key and others maintained, issue voting would also increase (Key 1966; Page and Brody 1972). Many of these researchers pointed to the more politically divisive 1960s as just such a period when issue voting should have been more prevalent (Nie, Verba, and Petrocik 1976; Pomper 1972).

Not all scholars are convinced that the political context can affect levels of issue voting. Some researchers have found that even when candidates emphasize their issue positions, issue voting increases only marginally (Margolis 1977). Additionally, the reported increase in issue voting in the 1960s was not accompanied by an increase in levels of issue constraint or political information (Converse and Markus 1979; Jennings 1992; Smith 1989). Further, although more voters may have believed that they were voting on the basis of the issues in the 1960s, they were frequently misinformed (Converse 1975).

In spite of these reservations, two related bodies of research seem to provide additional support for Key and his defenders. One group of scholars, referred to in chapter 1, finds that when the news media concentrate on a particular issue or set of issues, citizens will then use these issues as a basis of presidential evaluations (Iyengar and Kinder 1987; Krosnick and Brannon 1993; Krosnick and Kinder 1990; Zaller 1992). The second body of research generally supportive of Key's intuition comes from the work on campaign effects. Although most scholarly work has found that campaigns do not produce dramatic conversion effects (although see Zaller 1996), incumbents' strategies can affect how voters perceive their issue positions (Franklin 1991). More importantly, campaigns can also "activate" the voter's latent political predispositions (Berelson, Lazarsfeld, and McPhee 1954; Finkel 1993; Gelman and King 1993; Petrocik 1996; Popkin 1991; although also see Bartels 1992, 1997). In short, campaign messages remind voters of how they "should" vote, given their partisan and social group attachments.

The early Columbia studies represent a case in point of how individual characteristics and external stimuli can interact to influence political judgments (Berelson, Lazarsfeld, and McPhee 1954; Lazarsfeld, Berelson, and Gaudet 1944). Lazarsfeld, Berelson, and their colleagues found that President Harry Truman's emphasis on class issues during the 1948 campaign had the effect of priming support among voters most concerned with this issue.[1] These results, although suggestive, are limited for a number of reasons. Most importantly, they focus on only one election, thus providing little assurance that their results were not somehow idiosyncratic to 1948. Consequently, although the Columbia scholars show that voters concerned about class issues became more supportive of Truman over the course of the campaign, they provide only indirect evidence that this occurred *because* of Truman's emphasis on these issues.

More conclusive evidence might show that such increases would not have occurred in the absence of class appeals by Truman.[2]

Building on the work of the Columbia scholars and others, this chapter argues that the joint effects of issue salience and contextual factors will significantly influence the vote choice. More specifically, citizens most concerned with an issue should differ from comparable citizens in two ways. First, the incumbent's voting record on labor issues, defense issues, or abortion will figure more prominently in their vote decision, irrespective of the cues present in the political environment. Second, the incumbent's record on these issues will become increasingly important to their vote decision as the issue becomes more prominent in the campaign.

Issue Salience and Issue Voting

Union Members and Labor Issues

We learned in chapter 4 that union members, and to a lesser extent individuals living in union households, were more likely than other respondents to recognize when labor issues were raised in Senate campaigns. However, are they also more likely to consider the incumbent's record on labor issues when casting their ballots? Moreover, do union members engage in more issue voting on labor themes, as these themes become more prominent in the campaign? To answer both of these questions, I relied on logistic regression analysis (described more fully in the appendix to this chapter). The results of this analysis were then converted into predicted probabilities as shown in table 5.1.

Table 5.1 presents the results for nonunion members, residents of union households, and union members for 1988 and 1992.[3] The probabilities presented in this table vary the record of the incumbent on labor issues and the prominence of these issues in the campaign.[4] Additionally, to generate the probabilities, values are assigned to each of the remaining coefficients. As our principal interest is in the impact of the incumbent's voting record and the prominence of relevant issues on different groups (i.e., respondents for whom an issue is salient and those for whom it is not), all other variables in the model are held constant at their mean or median. In practice, this means that our predicted probabilities in tables 5.1 through 5.4 are based on ideologically moderate independents with average views of the state of the economy and average approval ratings for the president.[5]

The first portion of table 5.1 shows the results for prolabor respondents who do not belong to a union or reside in a union household.[6]

Table 5.1
Predicted Probability of Voting for Incumbent, by Union Membership and
Residence in Union Household (1988 and 1992)

| COPE Score | Nonunion Members | | |
	Labor Issues Not Prominent	Labor Issues Somewhat Prominent	Labor Issues Very Prominent
High (100)	.77	.77	.77
75	.71	.72	.73
25	.55	.59	.63
Low (0)	.46	.52	.57

| COPE Score | Union Households | | |
	Labor Issues Not Prominent	Labor Issues Somewhat Prominent	Labor Issues Very Prominent
High (100)	.65	.90	.98
75	.59	.83	.94
25	.47	.57	.66
Low (0)	.41	.41	.40

| COPE Score | Union Members | | |
	Labor Issues Not Prominent	Labor Issues Somewhat Prominent	Labor Issues Very Prominent
High (100)	.64	.90	.98
75	.47	.80	.95
25	.17	.41	.70
Low (0)	.09	.23	.46

Source: 1988-1992 Senate Election Study.
Note: Probabilities are based on logistic regression analyses presented in table 5A.

The best way to read the table is one column at a time. The first column reports the probability that these respondents would vote for senators of varying levels of policy responsiveness to organized labor, as indicated on the left side of the table, *in states where labor themes were not mentioned.* Not surprisingly, prolabor citizens who are not affiliated with unions are nevertheless more likely to vote for senators as their track record on labor issues becomes increasingly appealing (i.e., as they move from 0 to 100 on the COPE index). More specifically, when their senator consistently opposes the position of organized labor, prolabor respondents have only about a .46 probability of supporting the incumbent, all else being equal. However, when this hypothetical senator consistently supports the issue positions of organized labor, the probability rises to .77.

This relationship between the incumbent's objective voting record and these citizens' probability of support is both substantively large and statistically significant.

The last two columns report how the probability of support shifts in campaign environments where labor themes are raised. For union families, whom we will examine shortly, increasing prominence devoted to labor issues should result in a stronger relationship between probability of support and the incumbent's record. However, for nonunion members, the effect should be much smaller. The results from table 5.1 support this expectation. As labor themes increase in prominence, the difference between the probabilities of support for responsive versus nonresponsive senators actually decreases (although this effect is not statistically significant). Clearly, citizens who do not belong to unions but who are nevertheless sympathetic to their concerns *do* consider incumbent's record on these issues at election time. They *do not*, however, become more likely to do so when labor issues are emphasized in the campaign.

The middle portion of table 5.1 presents the probabilities for residents of union households (i.e., union members *and* the relatives of union members). Examining the first column, we find that the impact of the senator's record on labor issues is roughly equivalent to the results described above. However, these findings do not reach conventional levels of statistical significance (see table 5A in the appendix to this chapter). In short, we cannot reject the hypothesis that, generally, senators' voting records have no impact on candidate support. These results change markedly, however, when labor issues become more prominent in the campaign. In states where labor themes are moderately prominent, the predicted probability of support for senators who score 0 on the COPE index is only .41 whereas the probability rises to .90 for senators scoring 100. In states where labor themes are highly visible, the probability of support increases from .40 to .98.[7] As hypothesized, campaigns do have the effect of priming voters, but only those voters, predisposed to accept the message.[8]

The lower portion of table 5.1 examines how union members respond both to changes in their senator's record on labor issues and the campaign environment. The results from the first column show that union members are very sensitive to their senator's actual performance on labor issues, even when they are not mentioned in the campaign. The probability that a prolabor union member will support senators with a 0 on the COPE measure is extremely low at .09. The probability of support for senators who consistently vote with organized labor, however, rises significantly to .64.[9] This .55 increase in probability of support is almost twice the size of the gain in support among nonunion members. This is consistent with my expectation that citizens more concerned with labor themes would be far more likely to evaluate senators based on their record on this issue. Interestingly, however, the presence of labor themes in the campaign does not appreciably affect this relationship, as shown in the final two columns. Support for senators scoring high on the COPE index does increase as labor themes become more prominent, but it also increases for senators who are not responsive on this measure. On balance, the difference between high- and low-scoring senators is unaffected by the campaign context. Context apparently does matter, but only for voters with moderately high levels of interest in labor issues.

Partisanship, Gender, and Defense Issues

We now know that perceptions of issue importance and campaign context can affect the strength of issue voting on labor themes. Republican men and Democratic women should also engage in more issue voting on defense policy than other voters, especially when this issue is emphasized in the campaign. The largely positive effects in the case of union members, however, may not be an indication of similar results for other groups. After all, unlike the other issue publics selected in this study, union members formally belong to their group and in many cases receive group-oriented political information as well as explicit instructions from their leaders concerning how they should vote. Partisan identifiers, however, rarely belong in any formal sense to a political party and do not typically receive "group" information beyond that provided by party labels. Moreover, levels of identifications with the two major parties have been in decline for some time. It is possible, therefore, that in this case group membership will not act as a suitable proxy for issue importance, and thus the level of issue voting will be weaker.

Table 5.2 presents the predicted probability of voting for Senate incumbents for each of the four gender and partisan groups. The probabilities are based on the likelihood that Democratic or Republican citizens would vote for senators belonging to their party with varying levels of support for defense spending.[10] The first half of the table shows results for Democratic women and men who do *not* support increases in military spending. In both cases, the results are largely flat in states where defense themes were not raised in the campaign. However, in the case of Democratic women, the campaign context has a dramatic effect on the probability that they will support the incumbent. When defense issues achieve at least moderate levels of prominence in the campaign, these voters are all but certain of voting for senators who consistently oppose increases in military spending. The probability of support for Democratic senators

Table 5.2
Predicted Probability of Voting for Incumbent, by Gender and Party
Identification (1988–1992)

| | Democratic Women | | |
NSI Score	Defense Issues Not Prominent	Defense Issues Somewhat Prominent	Defense Issues Very Prominent
High (100)	.82	.70	.54
75	.83	.79	.75
25	.86	.91	.95
Low (0)	.87	.95	.98

| | Democratic Men | | |
NSI Score	Defense Issues Not Prominent	Defense Issues Somewhat Prominent	Defense Issues Very Prominent
High (100)	.83	.87	.90
75	.84	.86	.87
25	.86	.83	.78
Low (0)	.87	.81	.73

| | Republican Women | | |
NSI Score	Defense Issues Not Prominent	Defense Issues Somewhat Prominent	Defense Issues Very Prominent
High (100)	.80	.96	.99
75	.81	.95	.99
25	.83	.89	.93
Low (0)	.84	.85	.85

| | Republican Men | | |
NSI Score	Defense Issues Not Prominent	Defense Issues Somewhat Prominent	Defense Issues Very Prominent
High (100)	.89	.92	.94
75	.87	.84	.80
25	.80	.51	.21
Low (0)	.77	.32	.06

Source 1988–1992 Senate Election Study.

Note. Probabilities are based on logistic regression analyses presented in table 5B. Results are for Democratic voters who either oppose greater defense spending or are neutral and Republican voters who favor increases in defense spending. The senators being evaluated are assumed to be Democrats in the case of Democratic voters and Republicans in the case of Republican voters.

who favor such increases becomes progressively lower as defense themes become more prominent in the campaign environment. In contrast, the effects for Democratic men run mildly in the opposite direction and, in any case, are not statistically significant.

The results for prodefense Republicans, shown in the bottom half of table 5.2, also conform to expectations. For Republican women, their incumbent's record on military issues has little significant effect on their vote choice—even when the issue is highly publicized. Republican men, on the other hand, are quite sensitive to this issue. When defense matters are *not* prominently mentioned in the election, these voters make only a moderate distinction between incumbents who support their position and those who do not. However, when defense issues are raised in the campaign, Republican men are much more likely to engage in issue voting. For example, when the probability of hearing of defense issues is about .5, the probability that Republican men will support prodefense Republican senators is over .9. The probability of support for senators who frequently oppose such policies, however, is roughly .3.

As with voters concerned about labor themes, voters with particular interests in defense policy are also more likely to vote on this issue than are other citizens. Unlike in the previous section, however, this result is as dependent upon the campaign context as it is on the attitudes of the voter. It is unclear why context seems to matter more for defense issues than for labor themes. It is possible, however, that the necessarily more organized nature of unions allows members to learn more easily of the voting record of politicians even when such information is not present in the campaign environment.

Gender, Religion, and Abortion

The final issue examined in this chapter is abortion. The expectation here is that women, especially upper-middle-class professional women, as well as the religious groups identified in chapter 4 will be more likely than other voters to consider the incumbent's record on this issue at election time. Since none of these groups is as formally organized as are union members, whatever issue monitoring that takes place should be heavily contingent on the campaign environment. That is, these groups should pay little heed to their incumbent's record on abortion issues unless the issue receives some attention in the campaign.

The top and middle portions of table 5.3 show results for pro-choice men and women. If the senator's voting record on abortion influenced the vote decision, then senators with higher scores on the NARAL measure would enjoy greater support than do senators with lower scores. We

Table 5.3

Predicted Probability of Voting for Incumbent for Pro-Choice Men and Women (1988–1992)

NARAL Score	Pro-Choice Men		
	Abortion Not Prominent	Abortion Somewhat Prominent	Abortion Very Prominent
High (100)	.68	.70	.72
75	.70	.70	.69
25	.74	.69	.64
Low (0)	.76	.69	.61

NARAL Score	Pro-Choice Women		
	Abortion Not Prominent	Abortion Somewhat Prominent	Abortion Very Prominent
High (100)	.73	.83	.90
75	.72	.75	.77
25	.70	.52	.34
Low (0)	.69	.40	.17

NARAL Score	High-Status Pro-Choice Men		
	Abortion Not Prominent	Abortion Somewhat Prominent	Abortion Very Prominent
High (100)	.80	1.00	1.00
75	.77	1.00	1.00
25	.71	1.00	1.00
Low (0)	.68	1.00	1.00

NARAL Score	High-Status Pro-Choice Women		
	Abortion Not Prominent	Abortion Somewhat Prominent	Abortion Very Prominent
High (100)	.73	.71	.69
75	.59	.49	.40
25	.29	.14	.06
Low (0)	.18	.06	.02

Source: 1988–1992 Senate Election Study.

Note: High status is defined as high education and high income. Probabilities are based on logistic regression analyses presented in table 5C.

see at the top of table 5.3 that results are weak or nonexistent for pro-choice men. In fact, the effects run in the "wrong" direction when abortion is not an issue in the campaign. As this issue becomes more prominent this trend reverses, although the effects are of only moderate size and statistically insignificant even when abortion is highly prominent.

Results for pro-choice women present a different picture. They are far more likely than men to take into account their incumbent's record on abortion at election time. For example, when abortion is not emphasized in a Senate campaign, pro-choice women make no distinction between incumbents who score high or low on the NARAL index. When abortion becomes moderately prominent, however, the probability that pro-choice women will support senators with consistent pro-choice voting records rises to .83, whereas the probability of support for senators with consistent pro-life records declines to .40. This .43 margin increases still further when abortion becomes exceptionally prominent. In these campaigns, the model predicts that the probability that pro-choice women will support senators with perfect pro-choice records is .90. Alternatively, the probability of support for senators who consistently oppose pro-choice legislation is only .17.

Although pro-choice men in general do not appear to take their senators' abortion record into account at election time, it is possible that those with higher levels of education and income react differently. Indeed, we know that higher socioeconomic status is associated with stronger pro-choice attitudes for both men and women. To determine if issue voting on abortion occurs more frequently among higher-status citizens, the analysis described above was repeated with upper-middle-class voters only. Among men of high socioeconomic status we see that none of the anticipated effects is present. High-status, pro-choice men are almost uniformly supportive of Senate incumbents, whatever their record on abortion. The results for high-status women, however, are quite different. Even when the issue is not raised in the campaign, the difference for these voters between senators who consistently support abortion rights and to senators who consistently oppose them is about 0.55. This tendency increases somewhat (although not significantly) when the issue becomes more prominent in the race. As in the case of union members, these results suggest that for some voters an issue can be so important that they rely upon it as a basis for political evaluations even when the candidates make no overt reference to it.

Another group of voters who are likely to care considerably about the record of their senators on the abortion controversy are Protestant fundamentalists and Catholics. We already know that they are more likely than other pro-life citizens to recognize when this issue is raised in the campaign. They should also be more likely than citizens with similar

Table 5.4

Predicted Probability of Voting for Incumbent for Catholics,
Fundamentalist Protestants, and Other Pro-Life Voters (1988–1992)

NARAL Score	Non-Fundamentalist Pro-Life Citizens		
	Abortion Not Prominent	Abortion Somewhat Prominent	Abortion Very Prominent
High (100)	.64	.75	.84
75	.65	.72	.78
25	.67	.63	.60
Low (0)	.68	.59	.49

NARAL Score	Pro-Life Catholics and Protestant Fundamentalists		
	Abortion Not Prominent	Abortion Somewhat Prominent	Abortion Very Prominent
High (100)	.68	.06	.00
75	.64	.32	.11
25	.56	.96	1.00
Low (0)	.51	.99	1.00

Source: 1988–1992 Senate Election Study.

Note: Probabilities are based on logistic regression analyses presented in table 5D.

views to vote on this issue. As with the other groups, the results of the logistic regression analysis (see appendix to this chapter) have been converted into predicted probabilities, as shown in table 5.4.

In spite of the very real passions aroused on both sides of this issue, the results of table 5.4 are remarkably consistent with those of table 5.3. The political decisions of most voters are unaffected by their representative's position on abortion.[11] More specifically, pro-life voters who do not identify themselves as fundamentalists or Catholic simply do not consider their senators' position on abortion at election time. Moreover, there is some indication that, as the issue gains attention, pro-life voters are more likely to support their incumbents as they become more *liberal* on abortion. This counterintuitive result falls just short of conventional levels of statistical significance.

Unlike pro-life voters generally, pro-life fundamentalists and Catholics do care about their incumbent's record on abortion, and it powerfully influences their vote choice. Interestingly, however, this is only true when the issue is raised in the campaign. When abortion is not an issue in the election (which is true for the vast majority of elections) *pro-life fundamentalists and Catholics are actually more likely to support senators with pro-choice voting records.* This does not necessarily mean that these voters are unaware of their incumbent's position on this issue in these campaigns. It does suggest, however, that when the issue is not present in the campaign, even these voters do not consider it sufficiently important to affect their vote decision.

When abortion does become an issue in the campaign, pro-life religious group members become exceptionally sensitive to it. For example, when abortion becomes at least moderately prominent in the campaign, the probability that pro-life fundamentalists and Catholics will support pro-choice senators changes from about .7 to essentially zero, while the probability of support for pro-life senators becomes all but certain. The effects are even more pronounced when abortion becomes extremely prominent in the election. As many have long suspected, pro-life fundamentalists and Catholics do care dearly about their representative's position on abortion. However, in most cases these concerns are only latent and await a priming stimulus from the candidates (or some other political elites) before they become activated.

Conclusion

This chapter has shown, as other researchers have also demonstrated, that voters can evaluate politicians on the basis of their performance on the issues. What others have not stressed, however, is that issue voting often relies heavily on both perceptions of issue importance and an amenable campaign context. This seems especially true for voters who have moderately high levels of concern about a particular issue. Citizens who live in union households, for example, or women in general seem to fit this description. These voters do indeed respond when their issues are prominently raised in the campaign, but when they are not mentioned, voters apparently judge the incumbent on other criteria.

A different result seems to occur for voters with an intense interest in an issue. For example, women of high socioeconomic status and union members evaluate the incumbent on the basis of their performance on issues they regard as important whether they are raised in the campaign or not. Taken together, the results from this chapter generally support the priming hypothesis but also suggest an important modification of the theory: Priming effects are more easily triggered among citizens already interested in a given issue.

Finally, my results show that the content of campaign messages can significantly affect voters. Previous work has typically been based on only a few contests at best and has found only modest or inconsistent effects. When examining literally dozens of relatively high-profile campaigns, however, I find that candidate decisions to emphasize (or not emphasize) particular issues can have considerable effects on the vote choice. Again, as the early Columbia studies suggested, these campaign appeals are more effective on voters predisposed to respond to the message.

Overall, my results underscore that V. O. Key (1966) was right when he wrote that voters are not fools. It is true that most citizens, even those interested in a particular issue, are not routinely attentive to their incumbent's stand on that issue. Still, when the issue is raised, interested voters become informed and are able to evaluate their incumbent based on reasonably accurate knowledge of his or her voting record. Thus, as long as political elites (e.g., candidates, interest groups, mass media) are doing their job of raising the important issues, interested voters can be counted on to do their job of holding politicians accountable.

Appendix to Chapter 5_____

Measurement Notes and Model Construction

Measuring Responsiveness

Determining how accurately senators represent their constituents' interests on labor issues, defense issues, and abortion requires a measure of citizen attitudes as well as some indicator of their senators' true positions on these issues. The Senate Election Study provides the former in the form of standard survey questions. The latter is measured with interest group voting scores. These scores are based on anywhere from twelve to twenty or more roll call votes and range from 0 to 100, with 100 indicating the maximum level of agreement with the preferences of the interest group. Although these indexes are not perfect, other researchers have found that they reliably capture legislators' underlying ideological preferences (Kingdon and Jackson 1992; Lublin 1997). The interest groups ratings that I use are the American Federation of Labor's Committee on Political Education (COPE), the National Security Index (NSI), and the National Abortion Rights Action League (NARAL).[12] The COPE and NARAL scores represent the position of liberal interest groups, whereas the NSI adopts a traditionally conservative or prodefense posture.

Modeling Vote Choice

The dependent variable throughout this chapter is whether or not the respondent voted for the incumbent senator. This variable is coded 0 if the respondent did not support the incumbent and 1 if he or she did. To test the hypotheses outlined in this chapter, I used logistic regression analysis because of the binary nature of the dependent variable. The primary explanatory or independent variables are the prominence level of the relevant policy as described in chapter 4; the respondent's attitude on the relevant policy dimension (i.e., labor issues, defense issues, or abortion); the incumbent senator's score on the appropriate interest group index; and a series of interaction terms. The interactions are included because of my expectation that issue voting will be more likely to occur under some circumstances rather than others. For example, I hypothesize that prolabor union members will be most likely to take their incumbent's position on labor issues into account at election time if labor themes are prominent in the campaign. The model can be presented formally as follows:

Vote for Incumbent = $a + b_1$ (Campaign Theme) + b_2 (Policy Attitude)
+ b_3 (Interest Group Score) + b_4 (Score × Attitude)
+ b_5 (Score × Campaign Theme) + b_6 (Campaign Theme × Attitude)
+ b_7 (Campaign Theme × Score × Attitude) + controls + e

Again, the b_3 coefficient captures whether respondents are systematically more likely to vote for senators who traditionally support the liberal position on labor policy and abortion, or the conservative position on defense. This variable does not take into account the respondent's position on these issues or whether they are emphasized in the campaign. The two-way interaction variables, b_4 and b_5, are designed to capture whether this effect is conditioned on a respondent's position on the issue or the prominence of the issue in the campaign, respectively. The three-way interaction variable, b_7, is designed to detect those citizens for whom issue voting is contingent on their position on the public policy measure, their incumbent's voting record on this issue, *and* its presence as a campaign theme in their state.

My expectation is that the two-way interactions and the three-way interaction will be substantively larger for groups for whom the issue is important and markedly less so for all other respondents. More specifically, I expect that the interactions will on balance be significantly positive with regard to labor issues for union members and nonunion members who reside in union households. Similarly, I expect that the interactions regarding defense will be positive for Republican men (and, to a lesser extent, Republican women) but negative for Democratic women (and less strongly for Democratic men). Finally, the interactions should be positive for female respondents with a pro-choice orientation on abortion and significantly negative for religious respondents who take a pro-life position. Controls are also included in all of the models for partisan and ideological disagreement between the voter and his or her senator, electoral competitiveness, perceptions of the state and national economy, presidential approval, party of the incumbent, and the interaction of approval and party.[13]

Table 5A

Logistic Regression Model Predicting Effects of Interest Group Scores and Campaign Issues on the Vote for the Incumbent, by Union Membership and Residence in Union Household (1988 and 1992)

	Nonunion	Union House	Union Member
Intercept	1.84***	1.62**	1.66*
	(0.31)	(0.67)	(0.95)
Labor campaign theme (b_1)	0.27	5.63**	1.55
	(0.97)	(2.65)	(3.71)
Prolabor attitude (b_2)	–0.65*	–0.65	–2.52*
	(0.34)	(0.80)	(1.46)
COPE score (b_3)	0.00	0.00	–0.00
	(0.00)	(0.01)	(0.01)
Score × Prolabor (b_4)	0.01**	0.01	0.03†
	(.00)	(0.01)	(0.02)
Labor theme × COPE (b_5)	0.01	–0.06*	0.00
	(0.01)	(0.03)	(0.04)
Labor theme × Prolabor (b_6)	0.20	–5.68†	0.55
	(1.71)	(3.96)	(5.70)
Theme × COPE × Prolabor (b_7)	–0.01	.10*	.01
	(0.02)	(0.05)	(0.07)
% predicted correctly	71.29	74.07	75.00%
Chi-square	360.01***	119.53***	72.40***
–2 log likelihood	1899.59	359.62	196.37
N	1693	355	196

Source: 1988–1992 Senate Election Study.

Note: Models also include party distance, ideological distance, campaign competitiveness, perceptions of the state and national economy, presidential approval, party of the incumbent, and the interaction of approval and party.

† $p \leq .10$; * $p \leq .05$; ** $p \leq .01$; *** $p \leq .001$ for one-tailed test, except constant.

Table 5B

Logistic Regression Model Predicting Effects of Interest Group Scores and Campaign Is
on the Vote for the Incumbent, by Gender and Partisanship (1988–1992)

	Democratic Women	Democratic Men	Republican Women	Republican Men
Intercept	2.67***	2.68***	2.04***	1.72***
	(0.32)	(0.39)	(0.39)	(0.42)
Defense campaign theme (b_1)	0.02*	–0.01	–0.01	0.01
	(0.00)	(0.01)	(0.01)	(0.01)
Prodefense attitude (b_2)	0.81	0.49	–0.05	0.01
	(0.80)	(1.21)	(0.48)	(0.52)
NSI score (b_3)	–0.005*	–0.00	–0.001	.006*
	(0.003)	(0.00)	(0.003)	(0.003)
Score × Prodefense (b_4)	–0.01	–0.00	–0.00	0.00
	(0.01)	(0.01)	(0.00)	(0.01)
Defense theme × NSI (b_5)	–0.0003**	0.0002	0.00	–0.00
	(0.0001)	(0.0001)	(0.00)	(0.00)
Defense theme × Prodefense (b_6)	–0.03†	–0.01	0.01	–0.04*
	(0.02)	(0.03)	(0.02)	(0.02)
Theme × NSI × Prodefense (b_7)	.0004	0.00	0.0003	0.0007†
	(0.0003)	(0.00)	(0.0004)	(0.0004)
% predicted correctly	75.06	77.28	69.06	73.67
Chi-square	164.42***	119.08***	106.67***	158.74***
–2 log likelihood	863.06	626.41	786.28	712.20
N	822	581	682	657

Source: 1988–1992 Senate Election Study.

Note: Models also include party distance, ideological distance, campaign competitiveness, percep
of the state and national economy, presidential approval, party of the incumbent, and the interactio
approval and party.

† $p \leq .10$; * $p \leq .05$; ** $p \leq .01$; *** $p \leq .001$ for one-tailed test, except constant.

Table 5C

Logistic Regression Model Predicting Effects of Interest Group Scores and Campaign Issues on the Vote for the Incumbent, by Gender and Social Status (1988–1992)

	Men [a]	High-Status Men [b]	Women [a]	High-Status Women [b]
Intercept	2.12***	2.03***	1.89***	1.17*
	(0.23)	(0.58)	(0.19)	(0.69)
Abortion campaign theme (b_1)	−0.02	0.66†	−0.06	0.18
	(0.09)	(0.45)	(0.07)	(0.33)
Abortion attitude (b_2)	0.37**	0.76	−0.08	−0.91*
	(0.17)	(0.76)	(0.14)	(0.49)
Interest group score (b_3)	0.00	0.00	0.00	0.01†
	(0.00)	(0.00)	(0.00)	(0.00)
Score × Attitude (b_4)	−0.004*	−0.01	0.00	0.02*
	(0.002)	(0.01)	(0.00)	(0.01)
Abortion theme × Group score (b_5)	−0.00	−0.008†	−0.00	−0.003
	(0.00)	(0.006)	(0.00)	(0.004)
Abortion theme × Attitude (b_6)	−0.15	2.80†	−0.21*	−0.36
	(0.15)	(2.21)	(0.12)	(0.43)
Theme × Score × Attitude (b_7)	0.003	−0.02	0.005**	0.004
	(0.002)	(0.02)	(0.002)	(0.006)
% predicted correctly	72.59	72.08	70.41%	75.00
Chi-square	367.60***	66.20***	343.55***	52.43***
−2 log likelihood	1695.60	254.63	2124.62	206.55
N	1,558	246	1,886	205

Source: 1988–1992 Senate Election Study.

Note: Models also include party distance, ideological distance, campaign competitiveness, perceptions of the state and national economy, presidential approval, party of the incumbent, and the interaction of approval and party.

[a] All cases.

[b] High socioeconomic status respondents only.

† p ≤ .10; * p ≤ .05; ** p ≤ .01; *** p ≤ .001 for one-tailed test, except constant.

Table 5D
Logistic Regression Model Predicting Effects of Interest Group Scores and
Campaign Issues on the Vote, for the Incumbent for Catholics, Fundamentalist
Protestants, and Others (1988–1992)

	Fundamentalists and Catholics	Others [a]
Intercept	1.66***	2.25***
	(0.24)	(0.19)
Abortion campaign theme (b_1)	–0.18*	–0.03
	(0.09)	(0.07)
Pro-life on abortion (b_2)	0.32	–0.09
	(0.41)	(0.27)
Interest group score (NARAL) (b_3)	–0.00	0.00
	(0.00)	(0.00)
Score × Pro-life (b_4)	–0.00	–0.00
	(0.00)	(0.00)
Campaign Theme × Group score (b_5)	0.00	0.00
	(0.00)	(0.00)
Campaign Theme × Pro-life (b_6)	2.37*	0.01
	(1.05)	(0.22)
Theme × Score × Pro-life (b_7)	–0.04**	0.00
	(0.01)	(0.00)
% predicted correctly	70.26	72.54
Chi-square	240.61***	495.05***
–2 log likelihood	1412.83	2373.92
N	1,244	2,174

Source: 1988–1992 Senate Election Study.

Note: Models also include party distance, ideological distance, campaign competitiveness, perceptions of the state and national economy, presidential approval, party of the incumbent, and the interaction of approval and party.

[a] Respondents who are neither fundamentalist Protestants, Catholics, housewives, or women of high socioeconomic status.

[†] p ≤ .10; * p ≤ .05; ** p ≤ .01; *** p ≤ .001 for one-tailed test, except constant.

Six

Issue Importance, Campaign Context, and Perceptions of Candidate Distinctiveness in Gubernatorial Elections

IN THE LAST three chapters, we have seen that perceptions of issue importance can significantly affect the political information voters receive as well as their vote choice. Thus far, however, our focus has been entirely on Senate incumbents. This chapter extends our examination of the effects of issue salience to include gubernatorial campaigns. Additionally, this chapter shifts focus from incumbents who are seeking to protect their political office to candidates competing for open seats.

The results in this chapter differ from previous chapters not merely in that they focus on gubernatorial candidates. As indicated more fully below, this chapter also provides an additional test of the theory outlined in chapter 1. We learned from chapter 5 that concerned voters do respond to their incumbent's actual voting record, and at times this effect is enhanced by how prominently the issue is discussed in the campaign. However, because of the limitations of the survey, we could not be fully confident that group members were supporting (or opposing) a candidate *because of their position on the issues.* One way to be more confident of this conclusion is to directly measure voters' *subjective* perceptions of the candidate's responsiveness to the issues they regard as important. The survey data examined in this chapter allow for just such a test.

Another distinction between this chapter and the previous ones is that we can explore more precisely the relationship between perceptions of issue importance and information gain. As in chapter 4, this chapter examines whether issue publics are more aware of relevant issues when they are raised in the campaign. However, unlike chapter 4, this chapter examines whether group members recognize *which candidate* is discussing the issue. Additionally, because of the inclusion of traditional political information questions in the data used for this chapter, we can also investigate the influence of general political sophistication and possible interactions between it and perceptions of issue importance.

Nicholas Valentino is the co-author of this chapter.

Table 6.1

Newspaper Coverage of the Issue Content of Selected Gubernatorial Campaigns

	California	Georgia	Illinois
	Los Angeles Times	*Atlanta Journal & Constitution*	*Chicago Tribune*
Article discusses issue			
Abortion	32%	3%	13%
Labor issues	22%	27%	26%
Article mentions candidate position			
Abortion	28%	2%	10%
Labor issues	18%	0%	13%
Number of articles	50	68	39

Source: Courtesy of LexisNexis.

The 1998 Gubernatorial Elections

The survey data relied upon in this chapter are drawn from the 1998 National Election Study (NES) pilot study (see appendix to this chapter for details). The most relevant characteristic of this survey for our current purposes is that it focused on gubernatorial contests in only three states: California, Georgia, and Illinois. Additionally, the survey contained a number of items, discussed more fully below, on abortion and labor issues. A content analysis was designed in order to describe the variation across states in campaign discussion of these issues (see appendix). These results are presented in table 6.1.

The upper portion of table 6.1 displays the percent of campaign coverage in each state that mentions issues related to abortion or organized labor. Abortion was particularly prominent in California (see column 1). Out of the fifty articles coded for this state, sixteen (32%) included references to the abortion issue. This finding is very consistent with the conventional wisdom about the California gubernatorial race. The Democratic candidate, Gray Davis, and the Republican candidate, Dan Lungren, took distinct positions on abortion rights, with Davis strongly in favor of abortion on demand and Lungren opposed to abortion under almost any circumstances. In addition, both made their stand a prominent part of their campaign platform (Barone and Ujifusa 1999).

In Georgia, on the other hand, discussion of abortion was virtually nonexistent in the race between Democrat Roy Barnes and Republican Guy Millner. Only 3 percent of the campaign articles coded in the general election discussed abortion. This is also not surprising, given that both the gubernatorial candidates in this state were pro-life. On abortion, the most unusual contest took place in Illinois. In this state, the Democratic candidate, Glenn Poshard, opposed abortions, even in the case of rape or incest (Barone and Ujifusa 1999). His Republican opponent, George Ryan, arguably ran slightly to the *left* of Poshard on abortion, supporting them in cases of rape, incest, and when the health of the mother was at risk. In fact, Ryan aired a series of ads charging Poshard with being too conservative on a number of issues.[1] This deviation from traditional partisan platforms might have stimulated additional coverage. The results in table 6.1 show that 13 percent of the coverage of the gubernatorial election contained references to the issue.

Coverage in all three states devoted a significant amount of attention to labor-related issues. Given the fairly broad definition of such issues in this analysis, these results are not surprising. Candidates in all three states spent some time talking about labor-relevant issues, such as school vouchers, campaign finance reform for donations from union treasuries, unemployment, and other typical mainstay issues for organized labor groups. Though the *Chicago Tribune* and the *Atlanta Journal* were slightly more likely to cover these issues than the *Los Angeles Times*, about a quarter of all articles in each newspaper at least mentioned an issue that would be relevant to organized labor.

These content analyses suggest different issue contexts for each campaign. However, the data presented in the upper portion of table 6.1 do not indicate how clearly the candidates' positions on these issues were depicted in the media. In other words, it is possible that an issue may have received prominent coverage without a concomitant increase in the clarity of candidate positions on the issue. To address this possibility, information was also collected concerning whether the candidates' positions were explicitly discussed in each article. These results are presented in the lower portion of table 6.1.

These results reveal additional information about how local media coverage may have helped citizens distinguish between the candidates on these three issues. On abortion, the results look quite similar to those described above. In California, 28 percent of campaign coverage in some way mentioned the candidates' stand on the issue. The figure was 10 percent in Illinois and only 2 percent in Georgia, where the candidates' positions did not substantively differ. Thinking back to the earlier results, we find that almost each time abortion was raised as an issue in each of these states, the candidates' positions on the issue were also discussed. This suggests that Californians might have been much better informed about their candidates' positions on abortion, compared to constituents of the other two states in this analysis.

On labor issues, coverage in California provided significant information about the candidates' positions. Nearly one out of five stories contained some reference to the position of at least one of the candidates. On the other hand, the coverage analyzed in the Georgia governor's race was completely devoid of specific information about where the candidates stood. This finding is true for Illinois as well, as only one in ten articles explicitly identified either of the candidates' positions on organized labor. These results provide a noteworthy contrast to earlier findings. While there was significant mention of issues that would conceivably be of interest to union members and organized labor more generally, only a fraction of these articles explicitly discussed candidate stands.

The results of this content analysis indicate several likely predictions regarding the effects of issue importance and perceptions of candidate distinctiveness on voting behavior in each state. First, survey respondents in California should have a more accurate sense than those in other states of the candidates' position on the issues of labor and, especially, abortion. Given the results from previous chapters, this should be particularly true for citizens who regard these issues as important. Finally, because there was less explicit discussion of candidate positions on these issues in Illinois and Georgia, perceptions of candidate performance on abortion or labor issues should be less powerful in these states.

Issue Importance and Attentiveness in the Campaign Context

Chapter 4 demonstrated that issue publics were more attentive than other respondents to campaign discussion of group-relevant issues. Because of the nature of the survey data, however, we could not ascertain whether or not these individuals were particularly receptive to messages from one candidate rather than another. In particular, we could not explore whether issue publics were most attentive to messages that were sympathetic or antagonistic to their interests or values. The 1998 NES pilot study survey, however, addresses this issue in a limited fashion. Although the survey does not ask about candidate discussion of labor issues, it does ask respondents whether each candidate discussed the issue of abortion.

Media scholars have examined whether citizens tend to be selectively attentive to messages they generally agree with (Graber 1993). Although scholars initially found this to be a plausible and persuasive argument, recent evidence has been somewhat mixed. The "cognitive dissonance" that researchers thought would discourage citizens from absorbing disagreeable information was probably overstated. Instead, media researchers now think that citizens are more likely to encounter political information that they agree with because of their relatively homogenous social networks (Graber 1993; Sears and Freedman 1967). If this is true, then

Table 6.2
Respondent Perceptions of Whether Gubernatorial
Candidates Discussed Abortion during Campaign

	Republican Candidate		
	California	Georgia	Illinois
No discussion	51%	77%	66%
Discussion	49%	23%	34%
N	400	401	402
	Democratic Candidate		
	California	Georgia	Illinois
No discussion	32%	72%	68%
Discussion	68%	28%	32%
N	400	401	402

Source: National Election Studies, 1998 Pilot Study.

group members should be most informed, relative to other respondents, about messages originating from candidates they agree with. They may also be more informed about the candidate whom they do not support, but this effect should be less prominent.

Table 6.2 presents the percentage of respondents who believe that each candidate discussed the issue of abortion, by state.[2] Regardless of the party of the candidate, respondents were far more likely to indicate that the California campaign emphasized issues of abortion rather than the other two campaigns. The Democratic candidate—Gray Davis—was seen as particularly interested in this issue, with over two-thirds of all respondents indicating that he discussed it. No more than a third of respondents in other states thought either candidate had discussed this issue. These findings map well onto the content analysis results presented earlier.

Since we know that the issue of abortion was more prominent, both objectively and subjectively, in California, the following analyses will focus only on this state. As demonstrated in previous chapters, the respondents who are most interested in this issue are women, especially women of high socioeconomic status, and Christian fundamentalists.[3] First we consider gender differences. If, as some media experts argue, citizens are more attentive to information that they tend to agree with, then there should be a gender bias in information gain, especially for the Democratic candidate. Further, this effect should be especially pronounced among higher-status citizens.[4] Figure 6.1 shows gender differences in attentiveness to the Democrats' discussion of this issue across different levels of education. At the lowest levels of education, women

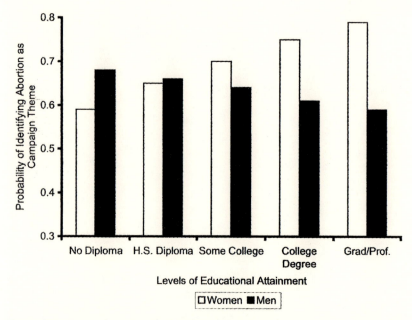

Figure 6.1. Predicted Probability of Identifying Abortion as a Campaign Theme for the Democratic Gubernatorial Candidate in California, by Education and Gender. Probabilities are based on logistic regression analyses in table 6A. (Source: National Election Studies, 1998 Pilot Study)

are less likely than men to recognize Davis's emphasis on the issue of abortion. However, at all other levels of education, women either reach or exceed the attentiveness levels demonstrated by comparable men.[5] Gender differences are especially large at the highest level of education, where the probability of attentiveness to this issue is .79 for women but only .59 for men.

Figure 6.2 presents similar results for the Republican candidate. Again, women with lower levels of education are far less likely than comparable men to indicate that Lungren discussed abortion in the campaign. This initial difference is, however, much greater than was the case for the Democratic candidate. As before, this gap diminishes as education levels improve. Still, this gender gap is never completely reversed until the postgraduate level. Moreover, even at this level, the advantage in attentiveness that women enjoy is not as great as in figure 6.1. Thus, perceptions of issue importance can compensate for women's generally lower levels of political knowledge, but the effects are greatest for the message they are most likely to encounter.

Unlike educated women, fundamentalist Christians should find themselves more likely to come into contact with the political messages of the

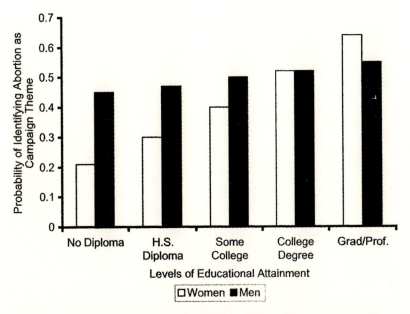

Figure 6.2. Predicted Probability of Identifying Abortion as a Campaign Theme for the Republican Gubernatorial Candidate in California, by Education and Gender. Probabilities are based on logistic regression analyses in table 6A. (Source: National Election Studies, 1998 Pilot Study)

pro-life Republican candidate, rather than the pro-choice Democrat. If so, then this group should be most informed, relative to other respondents, about Lungren's discussion of abortion. These expectations are largely confirmed, as shown in figure 6.3. Holding a number of plausible control variables constant, the average nonfundamentalist in California has a .43 probability of recognizing Lungren's discussion of abortion. This probability rises to .56 for fundamentalist Christians. In contrast, differences between fundamentalists and nonfundamentalists in perceptions of the Democrat's discussion of abortion are not significant (see table 6A, column 1 in the appendix to this chapter).[6]

Measuring Perceptions of Group Responsiveness

The previous section demonstrated that perceptions of issue importance are associated with enhanced attentiveness to gubernatorial candidates' discussion of abortion. This section explores the determinants and consequences of perceptions of candidate distinctiveness. Specifically, I examine whether individuals who regard a set of group-relevant issues as

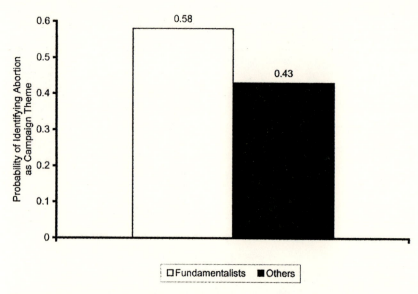

Figure 6.3. Predicted Probability of Identifying Abortion as a Campaign Theme for the Republican Gubernatorial Candidate in California, by Religion. Probabilities are based on logistic regression analyses in table 6A. (Source: National Election Studies, 1998 Pilot Study)

important are also more likely to perceive candidate differences on this dimension. These perceptions are important because, as indicated in previous chapters, they represent one of the criteria necessary for issue voting. The other requirements are awareness of the issue, a perception that the issue is important, and some discussion of the issue in the campaign context (Campbell et al. 1960; Key 1966). This section examines whether the combination of these factors influenced voting decisions in selected gubernatorial contests.

Given the campaign descriptions provided above, perceptions of candidate distinctiveness should be most pronounced in California, for two reasons. First, the candidates seemed to differ ideologically on a wider range of issues (abortion, education, labor, etc.) in California than in the other two states. Second, in California, the candidates' issue positions adhered more closely with their national party images. This is important because, in California, the candidates' platforms and their national party images both convey the same message as to which groups they favor. In Georgia and especially Illinois, however, the candidates and the national parties are sending out conflicting messages. Consequently, there should be less certainty about which issues and which groups the candidates support in these two states.

Table 6.3

Mean Group Responsiveness Score for Each State for All Respondents, Partisans, Informed Respondents, and Group Members

	Labor Unions				
	All Cases	Republicans	Democrats	Most Informed	Union Household
California	.42	.44	.45	.50	.54
Illinois	.09	.01	.25	.23	.24
Georgia	.13	.05	.20	.25	.11
(F-statistic)	(20.80***)	(15.19***)	(5.59**)	(9.07***)	(4.27**)

	Pro-Life Groups				
	All Cases	Republicans	Democrats	Most Informed	Christian Fundamentalists
California	–0.08	–0.10	–0.07	–0.22	–0.44
Illinois	–0.14	–0.28	0.02	–0.14	–0.19
Georgia	–.09	–0.32	0.07	–0.18	–0.14
(F-statistic)	(0.5676)	(3.47*)	(1.53)	(0.5292)	(3.29*)

Source: National Election Studies, 1998 Pilot Study.

Note: Perceptions of group-responsiveness run from -1 to 1. Positive values indicate that more respondents, on balance, view the Democratic candidate as better able to represent the interests of the group. Negative values indicate that the Republican candidate is seen as better able to represent the interests of the group. Values closer to 0 indicate that respondents see little difference between the two candidates on this issue.

* $p \le .05$; ** $p \le .01$; *** $p \le .001$.

Table 6.3 reports the mean perception of group responsiveness across each state for all respondents (see column 1). Positive values suggest that, on average, respondents perceived the Democratic candidate as a "better" representative of a particular group's interest (see appendix to this chapter for specific question wording). Negative values indicate the reverse, and values closer to 0 demonstrate either that, on average, neither candidate was perceived as more responsive or that there was little consensus among respondents. The top panel of table 6.3 reports the results for labor unions, while the lower panel provides the findings for pro-life groups.

The first thing that is clear from this table is that, with respect to labor unions, the Democratic candidate in California was generally seen as the candidate best able to represent this group's interests. Interestingly, however, this perception does not hold with regard to pro-life groups. In spite of the attention this issue received in California, most Californians do not view Lungren as unambiguously more supportive of pro-life groups than Davis. This may indicate that Lungren delivered his pro-life message to more targeted audiences given the generally pro-choice attitudes of the electorate. Whatever the reason, there is little difference in perceptions across the three campaigns for this more Republican group. Overall, the Republican is seen as being only marginally more responsive than the Democrat to the interests of pro-life groups.

The second and third columns in table 6.3 provide the average perceptions for Republicans and Democrats, respectively. The aim here is to determine whether respondents' perceptions were driven primarily by their party affiliation. If these questions are capturing something other than mere partisan biases, then regardless of party, respondents should view Democratic candidates as more responsive to the "Democratic" interest group (i.e., labor unions), and Republican candidates as more responsive to the "Republican" group (i.e., pro-life groups). This is, of course, assuming that the candidates adopt traditional Democratic and Republican positions on the issues. Since we know that this was more likely in California than in Illinois or Georgia, partisan agreement should be greatest in this state.

These expectations are generally borne out. For example, Republicans and Democrats in California agree that Davis is a much better representative than Lungren of organized labor. In fact, Democrats and Republicans have almost identical perceptions. In Illinois and Georgia, Democrats also perceive their party's candidate as the better representative of labor unions. However, Republicans in these states are generally more neutral than in California. Finally, there is also more agreement in California across party with perceptions for the traditionally Republican pro-life groups. In California, Democrats and Republicans viewed pro-life groups as best represented by the Republican candidate, whereas in the other states Democratic respondents were either neutral or slightly more likely to view their candidate as the better representative.

The fourth and fifth columns examine whether perceptions of candidate responsiveness to groups are significantly different for respondents who are likely to provide more accurate answers. These respondents are those scoring in the top half of the sample on the political information scale, and those who either belong to the interest groups in question or are likely to sympathize with their cause.[7] Beginning with labor unions, I find that the more politically informed, as well as union members, agree with other respondents that the Democrat is the more responsive candidate. The differences across each of the gubernatorial campaigns are somewhat more pronounced for more informed respondents.

With regard to pro-life groups, more informed individuals are somewhat more likely to view the Republican as better for this group (see the fourth column). However, differences across campaigns remain statistically insignificant. Christian fundamentalists, in contrast, have an entirely different view of the California contest. These respondents are far more likely than any other subgroup to perceive Lungren as the clear-cut choice to represent the interests of pro-life groups. This result is consistent with the findings of the previous section, wherein we found that fundamentalists were also more likely to learn of Lungren's pro-life message.

Perceptions of Group Responsiveness and Expected Vote Choice

We have seen from the preceding analyses that citizens do view the candidates as differentially responsive to interest groups. Moreover, as one might expect, these perceptions are at least partially contingent on the candidates' actual group-relevant issue positions. I now turn to an examination of the relationship between these attitudes and expected vote choice. This section explores whether the *perception* that a candidate is responsive to a group to which an individual attaches importance affects the vote choice. Note that this question differs from the one examined in chapter 5, where the focus was on the incumbent's *objective* responsiveness to a particular set of issues.

The impact of perceptions of responsiveness to labor groups is shown in figure 6.4 (see also table 6B in the appendix to this chapter).[8] These results apply only to California. Among individuals who do not reside in union homes, these perceptions have only a slight effect on candidate preference. When these respondents see no difference between the candidates, the Democrat enjoys a slight advantage, all else equal. When the Democrat is viewed as the more effective representative of labor issues, this advantage doubles but is still relatively mild.

Union households respond much differently to the perception of candidate responsiveness to their group. When the candidates are seen as interchangeable, these respondents lean toward the Republican candidate. This tendency more than reverses itself when the Democratic candidate is viewed as doing a better job for the group. Clearly, this perception plays a significant role in candidate preference. However, the effects are far greater for individuals concerned about the welfare of this group. Not shown in this figure are the effects for those relatively few respondents who thought the Republican would best represent labor unions.[9] Contrary to expectations, these results are also significant (see table 6B, column 1). However, these effects are not enhanced by perceptions of issue importance.[10]

The results of similar analyses for pro-life groups are shown in figure 6.5. Again, respondents who are likely to attach less importance to pro-life groups seem largely unaffected by the perceptions of candidate responsiveness to this constituency (see table 6B, column 2). For Christian fundamentalists, however, these perceptions are critically linked to their

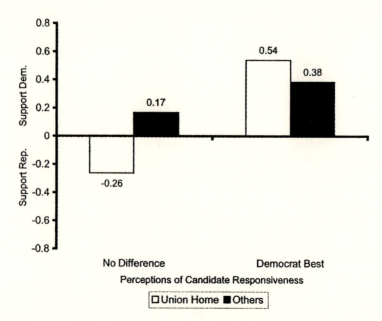

Figure 6.4. Relationships among Union Household, Perceptions of Candidate Responsiveness to Unions, and Intensity of Support for Gubernatorial Candidates in California. Point estimates are based on regression analyses in table 6B. (Source: National Election Studies, 1998 Pilot Study)

vote choice. When these respondents see no difference between the candidates, they tend to prefer the Democratic candidate for governor. When the Republican candidate is perceived as doing a better job for pro-life groups, these respondents—*but not others*—swing heavily in favor of Lungren. As with labor groups, the perception that the Democratic candidate would do better for these groups is also significant. The magnitude of these effects is relatively mild, however, and not significantly greater for Christian fundamentalists.

The interaction of perceptions of candidate responsiveness and issue importance clearly matters in a campaign context where the candidates gave priority to the relevant issues. Are these attitudes also important in contests that do not highlight these issues? Tables 6C and 6D, in the appendix to this chapter, provide an answer to this question. In Georgia, neither interaction significantly affects the vote choice. In the case of pro-life groups, the effects of these perceptions are also substantively small. For labor groups, however, there is evidence that respondents in general who regarded the Republican as more effective were also more likely to vote for this candidate. This is somewhat surprising as the Re-

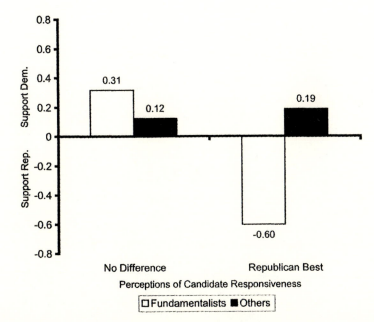

Figure 6.5. Relationships among Religious Affiliation, Perceptions of Candidate Responsiveness to Pro-Life Groups, and Intensity of Support for Gubernatorial Candidates in California. Point estimates are based on regression analyses in table 6B. (Source: National Election Studies, 1998 Pilot Study)

publican candidate, Guy Millner, is a mainstream conservative and unlikely to be a strong supporter of organized labor. It is possible that the campaign's silence on these issues (see table 6.1) may have simply invited some respondents to project their own attitudes onto their preferred candidate.

Results in the Illinois contest also suggest the importance of the campaign context. Recall that there was no clear indication as to which candidate was the more conservative on abortion in this election. Consequently, it comes as no surprise that the perception that both the Democrat *and* the Republican would best represent pro-life groups has a statistically significant and largely equivalent impact on the vote choice. Similar results emerge for labor unions. However, as in Georgia, in neither case is the combination of issue importance (i.e., group membership) and perceptions of group responsiveness a strong predictor of candidate preference. In short, even when the candidates do not highlight group-relevant issues, the latter may still influence political judgments. However, absent the appropriate political context, they do not have a distinctive effect on voters most concerned with these issues.

Conclusion

The principal aim of this chapter was to understand the way that information flows during campaigns might affect the criteria voters use to evaluate candidates. Specifically, I sought to show that attitudes about groups do affect political evaluations, particularly when the voter cares about the group. Additionally, this chapter sought to determine whether the objective campaign environment would affect information levels about candidate issues themes. Moreover, we revisited the issue, first explored in chapter 3, as to whether perceptions of issue importance and campaign context work interactively to enhance information levels.

Overall, these expectations were strongly confirmed. In California, where the candidates' positions on abortion were raised most prominently, voters were more clearly aware that these positions were being discussed in the media. In addition, respondents who were most interested in the abortion debate were also most attentive to the discussion of this issue. This was especially true for the messages to which respondents were most likely to be exposed. The campaign context also affected individuals' perceptions of candidate responsiveness to specific groups. When the information was available, respondents were able to identify correctly the candidates' positions on issues related to organized labor and pro-life groups. More informed respondents and individuals likely to care about these issues were even better able to make these distinctions.

The gubernatorial contest in California was the election in which the candidates were most distinctive on the issues. In this campaign, respondents from both parties were in agreement about which candidate would best represent union members and pro-life groups. These findings suggest that, at least in California, the campaign context gave clear enough signals that people were able to make informed choices with regard to these few issues. In Illinois and Georgia, however, either the candidates did not discuss issues involving labor and abortion, or their positions were effectively identical.

Finally, this chapter showed that the campaign context activated perceptions of candidate distinctiveness as a criterion in the vote choice among issue publics. In California, individuals from union households who viewed Gray Davis as a better representative for labor groups were far more likely than others to support him. Conversely, individuals from union homes who saw no difference between the candidates tended to favor Lungren. Similarly, Christian fundamentalists who viewed Lungren as likely to do a better job for pro-life groups were far more likely to vote for him relative to nonfundamentalists who shared this view and fundamentalists who did not.

In general, these results paint a fairly nuanced picture of the complicated ways that campaign context, issue importance, and candidate issue distinctiveness interact to produce candidate support. Of course, this chapter focuses on only a small number of states and a small number of issues. Still, when coupled with the results of the two previous chapters, this analysis demonstrates persuasively that, under the right circumstances, the electorate can behave in a far more sophisticated fashion than they have often been given credit for.

*Appendix to Chapter 6*_____

Measurement Notes and Model Construction

Unlike in previous chapters, the survey data in this chapter focuses on only three of the thirty-four gubernatorial elections taking place in 1998. The 1998 NES pilot study, which began on September 8 and ended on November 3 of that year, was designed to field new questions that might be appropriate for the scheduled 2000 study. Since the NES typically places its emphasis on presidential campaigns, the NES Governing Board thought that gubernatorial contests would most closely approximate this type of election. Because of financial considerations and the desire to study campaign effects more accurately, the decision was made to focus on three states rather than randomly sample citizens from all of the gubernatorial elections. The states selected were California, Georgia, and Illinois.

All of these states had at least one thing in common: there would be no incumbent seeking election for the governor's office. This characteristic is important because campaigns for "open" seats are generally more competitive, and the 2000 presidential contest would also not involve an incumbent. The particular states selected also provided regional, cultural, and ideological variation. The 1998 NES pilot study included approximately 400 randomly selected citizens from each state, with a combined total of 1,203 respondents.[11]

To understand the campaign environment in the states sampled in the 1998 Study, a content analysis was conducted of campaign coverage in the major newspapers of each state. These were the *Los Angeles Times* for California, the *Chicago Tribune* for Illinois, and the *Atlanta Journal & Constitution* for Georgia. Articles were randomly selected from the three months prior to the general election in each state. Two trained coders read each article from each state and coded whether or not an issue was mentioned. The reliability of the coding was quite high, with coders agreeing over 95 percent of the time on the presence of a given issue in an article, as well as the presence of specific candidate positions.

In each article, the presence of any discussion related to abortion, including partial-birth legislation, support from pro-life or pro-choice groups for either candidate, and mentions of the issue generally were coded as abortion related. Labor-related issues included any mention of organized labor groups, either specific or in general, and more general discussions of unemployment, school vouchers, teacher testing, union-ization for medical professionals, and campaign finance reforms with regard to union treasury funds. Vouchers and teacher testing were included under the labor category because teachers' unions strongly oppose these issues. These categories also captured general references to each issue without specific mention of candidate stands.

Group Responsiveness Questions

The specific survey questions used to measure perceptions of candidate responsiveness to groups are described below:

1. Now thinking about both candidates, do you think that CANDIDATE #1 or CANDIDATE #2 would do a better job for labor unions such as the AFL-CIO?

2. Do you think CANDIDATE #1 or CANDIDATE #2 would do a better job for prolife groups such as the National Right to Life Committee?

Each of the group responsiveness questions was recoded so that it would only have the following values: −1, 0, and 1. The negative value indicates that the respondent believes the Republican candidate would do a better job for the relevant group, whereas positive values indicate that the Democratic candidate is perceived as better. In addition to selecting either candidate, respondents were also given the option of "don't know" or refusing.[12] Individuals adopting these responses were coded at 0.

Group Responsiveness, Issue Importance, and Vote Choice

The dependent variable for these analyses is the respondent's *expected* vote choice. Their self-reported vote choice could not be used because the 1998 NES pilot study went into the field before the gubernatorial elections. The expected vote choice captures both the direction and the intensity of the respondent's candidate preference. It is operationalized as their partisan preference as well as how strongly they support the candidate. The variable ranges from −2 to 2, with lower values indicating a strong preference for the Republican candidate and higher values indicating a strong preference for the Democrat. Additionally, this variable excludes respondents who report that they do not intend to vote in the upcoming election.[13]

The principal independent variable is the group responsiveness question. The OLS regression model also includes controls for party identification, ideology, age, gender, race, education, and whether the respondent read about the campaign in the newspaper or followed it on local television. The group responsiveness variable was transformed into two dummy variables, each coded 0–1. One dummy variable represented the belief that the Democratic candidate would do a better job for the group, and the other represented the perception that the Republican candidate would best represent the group.

As in previous chapters, measures of issue importance were also included in the analysis. When examining perceptions of responsiveness to organized labor, issue importance is measured with residence in a union household. Approximately 20 percent of the sample resided in union households in California. This figure is 9 percent and 18 percent in Georgia and Illinois, respectively. When the dependent variable concerns pro-life groups, issue importance is measured with self-identification as a Christian fundamentalist. These respondents made up 18 percent of the sample in California, 29 percent in Georgia, and 25 percent in Illinois. Finally, terms were added for the interaction of issue importance and each of the group responsiveness dummy variables. The idea behind these interaction terms was that the impact of perceptions of group responsiveness would be greater for individuals who regard these groups as important. Formally, the model can be described as follows:

Expected Vote Choice = $a + b_1$ (Issue Importance) + b_2 (Democrat Best) + b_3 (Republican Best) + b_4 (Importance × Dem. Best) + b_5 (Importance × Rep. Best) + (Controls) + e

To the extent that the candidates adhere to national party images, the b_4 coefficient should be positive and significant for the "Democratic" group, and the b_5 coefficient should be negative and significant for the "Republican" group.

Table 6A

Logistic Regression Model Predicting Awareness of Candidate Discussion of Abortion in California

	Democratic Candidate	Republican Candidate
Constant	−0.13	−1.13*
	(0.58)	(0.56)
Female	−0.75	−1.47**
	(0.65)	(0.64)
Education	−0.10	0.10
	(0.14)	(0.13)
Female × Education	.35*	0.37*
	(0.20)	(0.19)
Fundamentalist	0.33	0.52*
	(0.33)	(0.30)
General political information	0.78*	0.14
	(0.41)	(0.38)
Partisan strength	0.29**	0.06
	(0.12)	(0.12)
Ideological strength	0.06	0.01
	(0.14)	(0.14)
Abortion attitude	-0.07	-0.11†
	(0.09)	(0.08)
Black	0.09	0.11
	(0.42)	(0.40)
Age	0.00	0.02**
	(0.01)	(0.01)
−2 log likelihood	479.661	521.356
Model chi-square	22.55	31.573
% predicted correctly	67.70	59.40
N	399	399

Source: National Election Studies, 1998 Pilot Study.

† p ≤ .10; * p ≤ .05; ** p ≤ .01; *** p ≤ .001 for one-tailed test, except constant.

Table 6B

Regression Model Predicting Effects of Perceptions of Group Responsiveness on Expected Vote Choice among California Respondents

	Labor Model	Pro-Life Model
Constant	−1.48***	−1.42***
	(0.31)	(0.32)
Union member *or* Religious conservative	−0.45[†]	0.18
	(0.29)	(0.31)
Democrat best represents group	0.20[†]	0.34*
	(0.15)	(0.18)
Democrat best × Group	0.58*	0.22
	(0.34)	(0.53)
Republican best represents group	−0.52**	0.04
	(0.21)	(0.18)
Republican best × Group	−0.62	−0.97**
	(0.54)	(0.38)
Adjusted R-square	0.45	0.48
Standard error	1.09	1.10
N	347	347

Source: National Election Studies, 1998 Pilot Study.

Note: Models also include controls for party identification, ideology, gender, race, age, education, whether respondent read about campaign in the newspaper, and how closely respondent followed campaign on local news.

[†] $p \leq .10$; * $p \leq .05$; ** $p \leq .01$; *** $p \leq .001$ for one-tailed test, except constant.

Table 6C
Regression Model Predicting Effects of Perceptions of Group Responsiveness on
Expected Vote Choice among Georgia Respondents

	Labor Model	Pro-Life Model
Constant	−2.46***	−2.54***
	(0.38)	(0.39)
Union member *or* Religious conservative	−0.14	−0.11
	(0.45)	(0.28)
Democrat best represents group	0.03	0.35*
	(0.17)	(0.20)
Democrat best × Group	0.52	0.28
	(0.57)	(0.39)
Republican best represents group	−0.81**	−0.47
	(0.19)	(0.19)
Republican best × Group	0.18	−0.11
	(0.62)	(0.36)
Adjusted R–square	0.41	0.41
Standard error	1.21	1.21
N	335	335

Source: National Election Studies, 1998 Pilot Study.

Note: Models also include controls for party identification, ideology, gender, race, age, education, whether respondent read about campaign in the newspaper, and how closely respondent followed campaign on local news.

* $p \leq .05$; ** $p \leq .01$; *** $p \leq .001$ for one-tailed test, except constant.

Table 6D

Regression Model Predicting Effects of Perceptions of Group Responsiveness on Expected Vote Choice among Illinois Respondents

	Labor Model	*Pro-Life Model*
Constant	−1.17**	−0.75
	(0.40)	(0.42)
Union member *or* Religious conservative	−0.11	−0.02
	(0.58)	(0.27)
Democrat best represents group	0.50**	0.53**
	(0.19)	(0.21)
Democrat best × Group	0.76	0.08
	(0.63)	(0.42)
Republican best represents group	−0.42**	−0.51**
	(0.19)	(0.19)
Republican best × Group	−0.09	−0.36
	(0.67)	(0.36)
Adjusted R–square	0.37	0.35
Standard error	1.25	1.27
N	334	334

Source: National Election Studies, 1998 Pilot Study.

Note: Models also include controls for party identification, ideology, gender, race, age, education, whether respondent read about campaign in the newspaper, and how closely respondent followed campaign on local news.

$p \leq .05$; ** $p \leq .01$; *** $p \leq .001$ for one-tailed test, except constant.

*Seven*_____

Issue Importance, Campaign Context, and Political Participation

THE PRIMARY GOAL of this book has been to specify the complex relationship among attitudes about issue importance, the political environment, what citizens know about politics, and how they vote. This chapter turns to a related yet equally important set of questions regarding the effects of the aforementioned variables on whether citizens participate in politics at all. Put simply, do factors in the political environment or attitudes about the relative importance of various issues encourage (or discourage) citizens to vote or engage in other political activities? As hypothesized in figure 1.1, it seems likely that the factors that influence how citizens think about politics would also be important for how they act on those thoughts.

To answer these questions, this chapter relies again on survey data from the 1988–1992 Senate Election Study, as well as the survey data drawn from the three states sampled in the 1998 NES pilot study. Contrary to expectations, I find that the interaction of context and issue importance has a less consistent effect on participation levels than it does on political knowledge and voting behavior. However, the survey data used in this chapter are not particularly well suited for this examination, and so my results are somewhat more tentative than in previous chapters.

Determinants of Political Participation

By "political participation," social scientists usually mean more than just the simple act of voting. They typically have in mind a series of acts ranging from voting to the more demanding task of contacting government officials or joining a political organization. Verba and Nie (1972), in their classic book *Participation in America*, develop a typology of four types of political participation. The first type is voting in national, state, or local elections. The second is campaign activity. This activity differs from voting because it is designed to increase a citizen's influence over the electoral process. Activities that fall under this definition include contributing money to a candidate or party, attending a political rally, working in a campaign on behalf of a candidate, displaying campaign signs outside one's home, or trying to convince others how they should vote. The other two modes of participation, "citizen contacts" (e.g., contacting government officials) and "cooperative participation" (e.g. joining a political group), involve activities unconnected to a specific campaign. Since this chapter is concerned with the effect of the campaign environment on political participation, the two latter forms of participation will not be considered here.

Research over the last several decades has identified a number of factors that are associated with political participation. The most consistent predictor is higher social status (i.e., education, income, and occupation). Among these variables, education is by far the most important (Wolfinger and Rosenstone 1980). In addition to demographic factors, a variety of psychological orientations are also associated with higher levels of participation. For example, researchers have found that feelings of efficacy or the belief that one can make a difference in the political process and that the system will be responsive to one's input can encourage greater levels of participation (Bobo and Gilliam 1990). One's level of interest in political campaigns can also affect participation levels (Verba, Schlozman, and Brady 1995).

Another set of variables that can affect participation rates, especially turnout, is factors in the political environment (Bobo and Gilliam 1990; Hansen 1997; Huckfeldt and Sprauge 1995; Sapiro and Conover 1997). Participation levels can be affected by, among other factors, the nature of the campaign (e.g., presidential elections draw more voters than congressional elections), efforts by the parties or candidates to get out the vote, or the characteristics of the candidates (e.g., a candidate's race or gender). Finally, Verba and his colleagues find that concern about specific issues of public policy can also influence participation rates (Verba, Scholozman, and Brady 1995).

Although much is known about the factors influencing political participation, little work has been done examining the *interactive effects* of issue importance and campaign environment. Two exceptions to this conclusion can be found in the work of Hansen (1997) and Sapiro and Conover (1997). In both cases, the authors examine the effects of female political candidates on citizen participation rates. Sapiro and Conover find that traditional gender differences in participation all but disappear when women are on the ballot. Hansen finds that women are much more likely to attempt to persuade someone how to vote when women candidates are present in the local political environment. An underlying assumption in the work of both sets of authors is that voters more interested in gender issues (i.e., women) will have greater motivation to participate when candidates sympathetic to those issues (i.e., women) are on the ballot.

This chapter extends the work of these scholars in the following ways. First, as is the case throughout this book, I look beyond one group in order to establish with greater confidence that perceptions of issue importance can affect political behavior. When examining the survey data on Senate elections, this chapter focuses on the groups identified in chapters 4 and 5. When moving to the gubernatorial elections, the focus shifts to women (especially educated women), respondents who live in union households, and Christian fundamentalists.

Another way this chapter builds on previous work is by measuring context effects in ways other than with the social group membership of the candidates. As before, the principal emphasis in this chapter will be on the issues that are emphasized in the campaign. Of course, the groups that candidates belong to often affect the issues they discuss in their campaign. Still, we do not know if previous results in this area derive from the presence of both group issues *and* group members on the ballot or just the latter. By focusing on the less obvious of the two, we can ascertain with greater clarity the effects of issue environment per se. If the interaction of context and issue importance matters, then each of the issue publics examined in this chapter should be more politically active when campaigns focus on issues relevant to their group.

Issue Importance, Context, and Voter Turnout in Senate Elections

Unfortunately, the 1988–1992 Senate Election Study did not contain the standard NES battery of questions on political participation. However, respondents were asked if they voted in the most recent Senate election. To determine if the issue environment affected turnout for relevant issue publics, I examine participation rates when the relevant issues receive "low," "medium," or "high" levels of prominence in the campaign. The percentage of respondents in each category and in each group is reported in table 7.1.

The top portion of table 7.1 presents the results for union members. In this case, the results conform to expectations. When labor issues are not present in the campaign (see column marked *Low*), union members and union relatives are no more likely than other respondents to report voting in the Senate election. However, when labor themes are moderately prominent, and especially when they are exceptionally prominent, large differences emerge. As expected, respondents with no union connection are mostly unaffected by the change in the issue environment. In contrast, respondents who reside in union households are about 20 percentage points more likely to vote, and union members are about

Table 7.1

Percentage of Respondents Voting in Senate Elections, by Group Membership and Prominence of Group Issue as Campaign Theme (1988-1992)

	Prominence of Group Issue as a Campaign Theme		
	Low	*Medium*	*High*
Labor Themes			
Union members [a]	66%	75%	100%
Union relatives [a]	63%	78%	83%
Non-union members [a]	64%	69%	68%
Chi-square	0.20	1.10	8.78**
Defense themes			
Women	62%	67%	68%
Men	65%	65%	74%
Chi-square	1.64	0.50	1.51
Republican women	67%	70%	67%
Republican men	65%	71%	73%
Chi-square	0.20	0.01	0.54
Democratic women	64%	70%	72%
Democratic men	68%	64%	75%
Chi-square	2.13	1.30	0.18
Abortion themes			
Women	63%	68%	65%
Men	65%	72%	70%
Chi-square	0.52	1.00	0.58
High-status women	83%	89%	100%
High-status men	80%	85%	100%
Chi-square	0.49	0.08	0.00
Pro-life fundamentalists and Catholics	59%	71%	50%
Others	64%	70%	68%
Chi-square	1.66	0.03	2.00

Source: 1988–1992 Senate Election Study.

[a] Percentages are based on 1988 and 1992 Senate elections only.

* $p \leq .05$; ** $p \leq .01$.

34 percentage points more likely to turn out. These changes are both substantively large and statistically significant. Moreover, the effects remain even when controlling for other factors associated with voter turnout (see table 7A in the appendix in this chapter).

Results for the other groups, however, are not nearly so strong. For example, the second group of respondents examined in table 7.1 comprises those presumed to have a special interest in defense issues. Among men and women, generally, men are only slightly more likely to vote than are women whether or not defense issues are prominently raised in the campaign. It is, of course, possible that subgroups among men and women were more affected by this issue in different ways, as indicated in chapter 4. However, when gender and partisanship are combined, the results remain unimpressive.

Similar results emerge for groups concerned about abortion. Among men and women overall, increasing the salience of abortion themes has little effect. Among high-status respondents (see chapter 4 for definition), the increasing prominence of abortion themes does seem to lead to an increase in turnout, but the effects are roughly equivalent for both groups. Additionally, both groups are so likely to vote, irrespective of the themes emphasized in the campaign, that any additional motivation provided by the presence of salient issues encounters a "ceiling effect." Finally, the increased salience of abortion themes also does not increase participation among pro-life fundamentalists and Catholics. If anything, the effects run in the opposite direction, although differences across the two groups are not statistically significant.

Issue Importance and Voter Turnout in Response to the Thomas Vote

Judging by the results described above, it would seem that the political environment does not consistently affect turnout among interested voters. The one exception to this conclusion is union members and, to a lesser extent, residents in union households. Higher-status respondents also seem to be moderately affected by the presence of abortion themes. However, their turnout rates are already so high that there is little room for improvement. Still, are there circumstances where these citizens might choose *not* to vote, in response to a set of issues in the political environment? Just as compelling issues or candidates may encourage turnout, the perception that the candidates are not exciting or, worse yet, disappointing may actually discourage voters from participating.

Measuring the perception that a political candidate disappointed a constituent is a difficult proposition. Certainly, the 1988–1992 SES carried no items that directly gauged this belief. Still, our discussion in chapter 3 of the politics surrounding the Thomas hearing allows us to identify a set of individuals who probably viewed their representatives as failing to live up to their expectations on issues of particular concern to them. These individuals are the liberal women constituents whose Democratic senators supported Clarence Thomas.[1] Although we learned in chapter 3 that these women were not significantly more knowledgeable about this vote than comparable men (although the differences were in the anticipated direction), it is possible that informed women were less likely to vote *if their Democratic senator was a supporter of Thomas*. In short, just as the expectation of policy responsiveness may encourage participation among some citizens, a perceived lack of responsiveness may also discourage participation (Bobo and Gilliam 1990).

Of course, instead of not participating in the election, liberal women could have simply voted against all supporters of Thomas, irrespective of party affiliation. The problem with this strategy, however, is that most supporters of Thomas in the Senate were Republicans. Liberal women could not plausibly punish these senators by withdrawing their support because they were not likely to support them in any case. The senators most likely to be politically damaged by the opposition of liberal women were the Democratic supporters of Thomas. Still, it is unlikely that liberal women would vote for the Republican challengers of these "swing Democrats." A second and more desirable option available to liberal women who knew how these senators voted and disapproved of their decision was simply not to vote at all.[2]

One way to test this hypothesis is to examine turnout rates among liberal women especially in states represented by Democratic supporters of Thomas. These rates are presented in table 7.2, along with the corresponding figures for liberal women in states represented by Democratic and Republican opponents of Thomas and Republican supporters of Thomas. For comparison purposes, results are also presented for conservative women in these states.[3] If the interaction of issue salience and context affected turnout rates in the 1992 Senate elections, then liberal women in states represented by Democratic supporters of Thomas should have been the least likely to vote. We see that this is indeed what happened. In general, participation rates hover between 60 percent and 90 percent across ideology and context. However, liberal women who were informed about this vote and who also were represented by Democratic supporters of Thomas were much less likely to turn out. This was true relative to conservative women in these states, and relative to liberal women in states with Democratic opponents of Thomas. Moreover, these differences remain even after controlling for all the traditional demographic and attitudinal variables associated with the act of voting (Hutchings 2001). At a minimum, these results suggest that the interaction of perceptions of issue importance and context can discourage political participation just as it can sometimes encourage it.

Political Participation in the 1998 Gubernatorial Contests

How did the differing political contexts of the 1998 gubernatorial contests affect participation rates? As in chapter 6, the answer to this question will necessarily be tentative given the limited nature of the survey

Table 7.2

Mean Turnout Rates in 1992 Senate Election by Ideology of Respondent and Partisanship of Incumbent (Women Only)

	Republican Senator			Democratic Senator		
	Opposed	*Supported*	*(F-Stat.)*	*Opposed*	*Supported*	*(F-Stat.)*
Did not know how senator voted						
Liberal women	62%	79%	(0.8293)	62%	—[a]	—
Conservative women	83%	74%	(0.2181)	78%	76%	(0.0514)
F-statistic	(0.6593)	(0.1564)		(2.6445)	—	
Did know how senator voted						
Liberal Women	—	78%	—	88%	50%	(7.27**)
Conservative Women	—	79%	—	80%	86%	(0.201)
F-statistic	—	(0.0096)		(0.6217)	(4.1958*)	

Source: 1988–1992 Senate Election Study.

Note: "Opposed" refers to senators voting against the Thomas nomination and "Supported" refers to Senators supporting the nomination.

[a] Entry has five cases or fewer in cell.

* $p \leq .05$; ** $p \leq .01$.

data. Specifically, only three states were sampled in the 1998 NES pilot study, so there is insufficient variance in political campaigns to reach strong conclusions in either direction. Still, one advantage that the pilot study data has over the 1988–1992 SES is that the former contains a full battery of questions designed to measure different forms of political participation. We also know from the rich content analysis data reported on in chapter 6 which policies were prominent in each of the three campaigns. Consequently, if the issue environment provides an incentive for interested citizens to participate, then respondents concerned about abortion (e.g., Christian fundamentalists and educated women) should have been especially motivated in California. Similarly, respondents interested in labor issues (e.g., residents in union households) should have been particularly inspired to participate in California and, perhaps secondarily, in Illinois.

The 1998 NES pilot study contained measures of six different kinds of political activity. Respondents were asked if they tried to persuade someone how to vote, if they engaged in acts such as putting a campaign sticker on their car, if they attended any political rallies, if they worked on behalf of a candidate or party, if they contributed any money to a candidate or party, or if they contributed to a political group. Each act had a range of 0–2, with higher values indicating higher levels of participation.[4] The six separate items were then combined into a "political participation scale" ranging, in theory, from 0 to 12. In practice, however, no

124   CHAPTER SEVEN

Table 7.3
Mean Levels of Political Participation in Gubernatorial
Elections, by Group Membership, across States

Participation Rates (0–10)	Illinois	Georgia	California
Union households	1.99	1.63	1.52
Nonunion households	1.05	1.03	0.87
Difference	0.94***	0.60*	0.65***
Women	0.90	0.90	0.87
Men	1.62	1.38	1.14
Difference	–0.72***	–0.48**	–0.27†
College-educated women	1.09	1.06	1.12
College-educated men	1.99	1.44	1.31
Difference	–0.90*	–0.38	–0.19
Christian fundamentalists	1.40	1.05	1.44
Other respondents	1.15	1.10	0.90
Difference	0.25	–0.05	0.54**

Source: National Election Studies, 1998 Pilot Study.
† p ≤ .10; * p ≤ .05; ** p ≤ .01; *** p ≤ .001.

respondent engaged frequently in all forms of participation. The actual range of this variable is 0–10.

Average participation rates, across groups and for each state, are reported in table 7.3. The first thing that is apparent from this table is that average participation levels are quite low for all groups. In fact, although respondents could score up to 12 points on this variable, the average score was closer to 1. Moreover, fully 57 percent of the sample did not engage in any of the acts described above. Still, the relatively low level of political participation is of less interest here than whether or not there are significant group differences consistent with my expectations.

Taking union households first, I find that although labor issues (and the candidate's position on these issues) were most prominent in California and Illinois, respondents in these households were more active in all three states. Moreover, contrary to expectations, differences between union and nonunion households were greatest in Illinois. The content analysis data in chapter 6 made clear that this issue was prominent in the Illinois campaign, but we know from the survey data that the perceived differences between the candidates were much greater in California. Why, then, were union households more politically active in Illinois than in California? Part of the answer may be a simple measurement issue. The survey data do not, unfortunately, allow one to identify respondents who belong to labor unions. The survey only asks whether someone in the household belongs to a union. We know that, compared with Califor-

Table 7.4

Percentage of Respondents Engaging in Any Acts of Political
Participation in Gubernatorial Elections, by Group
Membership, across States

Participation Rates (0–1)	Illinois	Georgia	California
Union households	0.56	0.46	.57
Nonunion households	0.42	0.41	.37
Difference	0.14*	0.05	.20***
Women	0.39	0.36	.38
Men	0.52	0.52	0.44
Difference	–0.13**	–0.16**	–0.06
College-educated women	0.40	0.41	0.49
College-educated men	0.58	0.49	0.47
Difference	–0.18*	–0.08	0.02
Christian fundamentalists	0.48	0.42	0.55
Other respondents	0.44	0.42	0.38
Difference	0.04	0.00	0.17**

Source: National Election Studies, 1998 Pilot Study.

† p ≤ .10; * p ≤ .05; ** p ≤ .01; *** p ≤ .001.

nia, a slightly greater percentage of Illinois residents are likely to be
union members.[5] Therefore, it is possible that the greater levels of participation in union households in Illinois are partially affected by the
greater density of actual union members.[6]

Turning next to the groups most concerned with the issue of abortion,
I also find mixed results at best. For example, given the singular importance of abortion in the California campaign, one might expect high
levels of participation among women. In fact, however, women are not
more active in California relative to other states. Nor are gender differences greater when focusing on college-educated respondents. If any
trend is evident, it is that men are considerably *less* active in California.
Only among religious conservatives do clear context effects emerge. Although this group was not particularly more active in California relative
to other states, they were much more active relative to nongroup members within California.

In table 7.3 participation rates were measured with both the number of
acts a respondent engaged in and how frequently they participated in that
act. Another way of gauging participation levels is simply to determine
how many respondents participated in any of the six political acts described above. This information is reported in table 7.4. When measured
in this way, we again find that participation rates were not high in the
three states sampled in the 1998 NES pilot study. On average, about 43
percent of respondents indicated that they performed at least one of the

six political acts. Are context effects more discernible when participation is measured in this way? For union households, the answer is yes. We saw in table 7.3 that across all three states union households engaged in a greater range and number of political acts than other respondents. However, we find in table 7.4 that a larger percentage of respondents in union households were active in Illinois and especially California, but not in Georgia. This is about what we would expect, given the lack of coverage of labor themes in the Georgia campaign. Among women generally, as well as college-educated women, the percentage of respondents participating in California is not especially great relative to men. Gender differences are slightly smaller in California than in the other two states, but the effects are mild at best. Finally, when participation is defined as the number of respondents participating in any political act, Christian fundamentalists were more active than others but, as expected, only in California.

Political Context, Group Membership, and Talking about Politics

Of the six political acts examined in this chapter, efforts to persuade someone how to vote are by far the most popular. Approximately 29 percent of respondents in the 1998 NES pilot study indicated that they engaged in this form of participation. In contrast, the next most popular activities were wearing a campaign button, putting a campaign sticker on your car, or placing a sign in front of your house (14% of sample). Less than 10 percent of respondents participated in most of the remaining acts.

Part of the reason for the relative popularity of political persuasion is that it does not require a tremendous investment of time or resources. This is important because women are often lacking in these areas compared with men, thus accounting for their somewhat lower levels of political participation (Burns, Schlozman, and Verba 1997). Equally important, Hansen (1997) has shown that the political context can affect women's propensity to talk about politics. In short, it is possible that the null results presented above for female respondents may not apply to what Hansen calls "political proselytizing."

To explore this possibility, I analyzed the political persuasion item separately from the overall political activity scale. This separate item ranges from 0 to 2, with a value of 1 indicating that the respondent attempted to persuade someone "once or twice" and a value of 2 indicating at least three attempts. The results for union household, gender, and religious affiliation are reported in table 7.5. Among union households, the greatest effects occur in California. Although labor issues were also present

Table 7.5

Average Score for Respondents Who Reported Trying to
Convince Someone Else How to Vote in Gubernatorial
Elections, by Group Membership, across States

Talking Politics (0–2)	Illinois	Georgia	California
Union households	0.56	0.54	0.70
Nonunion households	0.44	0.46	0.37
Difference	0.12	0.08	0.33***
Women	0.36	0.36	0.40
Men	0.59	0.64	0.49
Difference	−0.23**	−0.28***	−0.09
College-educated women	0.41	0.46	0.47
College-educated men	0.73	0.58	0.50
Difference	−0.32*	−0.12	−0.03
Christian fundamentalists	0.56	0.54	0.65
Other respondents	0.43	0.44	0.39
Difference	0.13	0.10	0.26**

Source: National Election Studies, 1998 Pilot Study.

† p ≤ 0.10; * p ≤ 0.05; ** p ≤ 0.01; *** p ≤ 0.001.

in the Illinois campaign, we know that respondents in union households were most likely to perceive the candidates as differing on labor issues in California. Thus, it is not surprising that they are also more likely to engage in political proselytizing in this case.

Surprisingly, however, effects for women are not significantly larger in California, where abortion was a prominent part of the campaign. Differences across gender are smaller in California, relative to the other two states in the sample, but this is primarily because few California men engaged in political persuasion. Similar results emerge among educated respondents. If there was any interaction between the issue environment in California and gender, then it resulted in decreased participation rates among men more so than increased rates among women. Lastly, the prominence of abortion themes in the California campaign was influential, but only for religious conservatives. Differences between Christian fundamentalists and other respondents on this dimension are at least twice as large in California compared with Illinois and Georgia.

Conclusion

The results of this chapter suggest that the relationship among issue importance, the political environment, and political participation is decidedly mixed. With regard to voting, only union members, and to a lesser extent respondents from union households, turn out in greater numbers when issues that they deem important are emphasized in campaigns. There are also some mild positive effects for high-status women, but this is also true of high-status men. Moreover, in both cases their turnout rates are so uniformly high that there is little room for any additional improvement as a result of the issue environment. For all other groups, the effects of the political context were weak at best.

Context effects were uncovered in the 1992 Senate campaigns among respondents concerned about the Thomas confirmation. Ironically, however, they did not act to increase participation among these respondents. Instead, respondents who were most disappointed in their senator's vote were motivated to avoid participation in the election. Clearly, under some circumstances, the political context can act to demobilize as well as mobilize some individuals.

The limited survey data from the1998 gubernatorial campaigns also indicate mixed support for the hypothesis that context can affect political participation. As anticipated, respondents from union households in Illinois and especially California were significantly more active than other respondents. Additionally, Christian fundamentalists were also more likely than other citizens to participate in a range of political activities in California, but not elsewhere. In both cases, issues relevant to these two groups (labor issues and abortion) were particularly prominent in the California campaign.

Unfortunately, women with a college education did not respond to the increased prominence of abortion themes in California with increased participation levels. This was true no matter how participation was defined. The latter finding appears to clash with some previous results showing significant context effects on participation rates among women. This earlier work, however, typically defined the political context in terms of the presence of female candidates (and the assumption that this was accompanied by an emphasis on "women's issues"). The results presented in this chapter suggest that a candidate's gender has a more powerful effect than the mere prominence of issues of disproportionate concern to women.

Finally, if any pattern has emerged in this chapter, it is that respondents with formal group affiliations are best positioned to take advantage of favorable issue environments. This was most clearly demonstrated with union members, but it also applied to Christian fundamentalists in the 1998 NES pilot study data. This dovetails nicely with the findings of other scholars that political and quasi-political organizations can be particularly effective at mobilizing their membership (Verba, Schlozman, and Brady 1995). What others have not emphasized is the important mediating factor of the political environment. In short, even citizens associated with an organized group will not necessarily participate in the absence of galvanizing cues in the political environment.

Appendix to Chapter 7_____

Table 7A

Regression Model Predicting Effects of Union
Membership and Residence in Union Households on
Whether Respondent Voted in Senate Election

	Regression Coefficient
Constant	−5.65***
	(0.33)
Union membership	0.10
	(0.09)
Prominence of labor theme	0.45†
	(0.32)
Union × Labor theme	0.86*
	(0.48)
% Predicted correctly	77.53%
−2 log likelihood	2442.831
Chi-square	822.302
N	2,577

Source: 1988–1992 Senate Election Study.

Note: Standard errors in parentheses. Models also include
controls for gender, race, age, income, education, political
sophistication, levels of political interest, whether respondent had contact with either the incumbent or challenger,
partisan strength, ideological strength, media consumption
habits, and the competitiveness of the election.

† $p \leq .10$; * $p \leq .05$; ** $p \leq .01$; *** $p \leq .001$ for one-tailed
test, except for constant.

Eight

The Role of Public Opinion in the Democratic Process

THAT THE mass public is typically uninformed and uninterested in policy matters has long been a settled question in public opinion research. This book does not dispute that conclusion. The implication that is often drawn from this characterization is that the American electorate may consequently be unable to carry out its democratic obligations. Here is where I part company with some previous work in this field. The expectation that ordinary citizens will routinely attend to political matters is more than just unrealistic, it is arguably elitist (Downs 1957; Mueller 1994). The insight underlying every chapter in this book is that all citizens need really do is obtain *sufficient* information on issues that they care about in order to cast an informed ballot at election time.

This book has focused on three central questions with the intention of rigorously testing this insight. First, are citizens provided sufficient political information to fulfill their democratic obligation to monitor, and subsequently evaluate, the performance of elected officials? Second, under what circumstances are citizens more or less likely to absorb this information? Finally, even if citizens do acquire this information, under what circumstances does it influence their political judgments? The answers to these questions are vitally important, for if it should turn out that citizens remain politically ignorant even under the most agreeable circumstances, then it will fundamentally challenge our view of representative democracy.

This book has argued that the best indicator of political engagement is individual motivation coupled with an environment conducive to the flow of adequate, and sufficiently compelling, amounts of political information. The foregoing chapters have tested this proposition by focusing on a variety of issue publics across a number of different political contests, at all times with an eye toward what citizens could be fairly *expected* to know. The survey data employed have not always represented the ideal test of the model, nor have the results always conformed to expectation. Nevertheless, the pattern of results has shown that, indeed, "voters are not fools" (Key 1966). Below I summarize these findings, as well as examine their political implications and speculate about possible avenues for future research in this area.

Overview

The Political Environment and the Mass Media

To assess the performance of the mass media, I examined an admittedly nonrandom sample of roll call votes in the House and Senate. The aim here was to determine whether or not the media, specifically major metropolitan newspapers, provide information on the voting records of individual members of Congress. Additionally, I examined why some votes receive prominent coverage while others do not. As it turns out, there is considerable variation in the manner in which newspapers cover different bills. However, the factors motivating this variation are predictable and consistent with the democratic obligations of the electorate.

Not surprisingly, I found that key votes in the House of Representatives and the Senate received far more prominent coverage than votes likely to be important to much smaller constituencies. For example, the authorization of force in the Persian Gulf War and the confirmation of Clarence Thomas both received significant amounts of coverage such that any interested reader could easily discern how their representatives voted. Alternatively, the confirmation vote for Judge Edward Carnes, Jr., to the Eleventh Circuit Court of Appeals and the extension of unemployment benefits in 1993 were poorly covered in the press even though many voters—and politically significant interest groups—regarded these issues as important.

Although more routine votes received less coverage, the media did provide more prominent information about the specific votes of legislators if they strayed from the position of the national party. Similar results were uncovered for members of Congress who adopted significant leadership roles on particular bills. In fact, in both cases, this was especially true of routine votes relative to key roll calls. An important exception, however, is that this applied only to the Senate and not to the House of Representatives. Apparently, the media regard the actions of individual senators as inherently more newsworthy than the actions of individual House members.

In practice, the less prominent and predictable coverage devoted to House votes means that constituents will find it much more difficult to monitor the record of these legislators. In theory, interest groups and political challengers might step in to fill the vacuum left by the absence of media reporting. Still, as indicated in chapter 2, this seems unlikely. Most interest groups simply do not have the resources to compete with daily newspapers in their ability to cover the Washington activities of local members of Congress. Political challengers, of course, have an incentive to provide this information, but relatively few House members face credible challengers. This does not mean that the theory outlined in figure 1.1 does not apply to these legislators. It does mean, however, that public opinion will be activated more infrequently in these contests.

Motivation, Environment, and Political Learning

Chapters 3, 4, and 6 examined the proposition that perceptions of issue importance and the appropriate political environment combine to produce higher levels of political learning. In the case of the Clarence Thomas confirmation vote, we found that blacks, conservative men, and, in a more limited fashion, liberal women demonstrated heightened levels of attentiveness to their senators' vote on this issue relative to their traditional levels of political knowledge. Context factors, such as the presence of female Senate challengers, were also associated with increased information levels. Moreover, in the case of African Americans, information levels were especially high in states where the fate of the nomination rested on wavering Democratic senators.

Although consistent with the model summarized in figure 1.1, the results from chapter 3 were limited in that they applied only to one high-profile vote. In chapter 4, however, we found that these results also held across a range of different issues, political contests, and issue publics. Examining dozens of Senate elections from 1988 through 1992, we found that union members, women (particularly those of high socioeconomic status), and Christian fundamentalists all demonstrated heightened levels of attentiveness when issues they cared about were raised in Senate or gubernatorial campaigns.

The relative influence of more narrow interests on political knowledge compared with more general interests also varied somewhat across the issues I examined. In some instances, such as the Thomas confirmation vote, measures of general attentiveness to politics were at least as good a predictor of information gain as were measures of issue salience. Interestingly, this was especially true for men. The general measure of political knowledge—with its emphasis on identifying national political figures—did not perform as well for women, perhaps suggesting that even women with a broader appetite for political news are, all the same, more interested in local politics.

In other instances, perceptions of issue importance were far better predictors of attentiveness than more general measures of political knowledge. This was particularly true in the 1998 California gubernatorial contest. In this campaign, Christian fundamentalists were much more aware than other respondents that Republican candidate Dan Lungren took a firm and very public pro-life position on abortion. However, the most attentive members of this issue public were not those who typically followed politics. Instead, fundamentalists who attended church most frequently were the most informed on this issue. Clearly, general attentiveness to politics is a good indicator that one will learn about specific political stories. Still, this example illustrates that, in at least some cases, intense interest (coupled perhaps with an organizational affiliation) can compensate for a general lack of political information.

More broadly, these results indicate that, although some voters are interested in a wide range of political stories, many others are attentive only when issues they care about are discussed. This provides strong support for the intuition of Key (1961), Converse (1964), and others who first developed the issue publics hypothesis. Further, these findings also indicate that the popular belief among politicians that the normally quiescent public is just one or two "wrong" votes away from becoming galvanized is not irrational. In short, just because the public is generally inattentive does not mean that they are *inherently* inattentive.

Motivation, Environment, and Vote Choice

Issues of individual motivation and the cues and information in the environment do not just interact to affect levels of political knowledge. They also influence how citizens vote. Evidence in support of this proposition was uncovered in chapters 5 and 6. For example, an examination of Senate contests from 1988 through 1992 featuring an incumbent showed that a senator's objective voting history on relevant issues affected the vote decision of constituents interested in those issues. As expected, environmental factors mediate this effect. However, this applied more to some groups than to others.

On the one hand, Christian fundamentalists, women, citizens residing in union households, and the combination of gender and partisan groups with strong views on defense issues were all far more likely to bring their policy preferences to bear on their vote choice *only* when relevant issues were raised in the campaign. In the absence of campaign discussion of "their" issues, these voters were perfectly willing to support incumbents who nevertheless opposed their interests or values. On the other hand, this tendency did not apply to women of high socioeconomic status and union members. These voters were apparently vigilant on issues they perceived as important whether or not they were raised in the campaign. Interestingly, each of these groups also tends to score high on general measures of political information. It is possible that the combination of broader political awareness and above-average levels of interest in a more specific set of issues lead to high and relatively stable trends of voter monitoring.

Chapter 6 showed that political judgments are driven not just by politicians' objective performance. Their subjective performance on relevant issues and their ability to represent particular groups are also important. Although this chapter focused on only three gubernatorial contests and perceptions of responsiveness on two groups, the results were quite consistent with previous chapters. Perceptions that a candidate would do a better job representing the interests of labor unions or pro-life groups were significantly associated with vote choice. This was especially true of citizens who are likely to regard these groups' objectives as important. Moreover, the political environment was an important mediator of this effect. When gubernatorial candidates, as in California, clearly indicated where they stood vis-à-vis group issues, the perception of group responsiveness among issue publics was strongly associated with their vote choice. In campaigns where the candidates' positions were murkier, this relationship did not hold.

As many others have argued, issue voting is not nearly as powerful, nor consistent, an influence on the vote choice as partisan identification. Indeed, in the vast majority of Senate elections studied in this book, issues likely to be important to union households, women, Christian fundamentalists, and partisans were not even raised. When they are raised, however, they can exert a dramatic impact on candidate evaluations. Politicians have, of course, long recognized this. Political scientists would also do well to acknowledge this and consequently incorporate measures of the issue environment into their models of voting behavior.

Motivation, Environment, and Political Participation

The joint effects of motivation and context on political learning and candidate evaluations seem both strong and relatively consistent. Motivation and environmental factors have a far more unstable effect on measures of political participation. As indicated in chapter 7, these results are more tentative than was the case in previous chapters. This is primarily because many of the variables necessary to conduct the appropriate tests are absent from the main surveys relied upon for this book. Still, the results that were reached were only partially supportive of the model summarized in figure 1.1.

Chapter 7 showed that union members and respondents who reside in union households are more likely to vote in Senate elections and participate in politics more broadly in gubernatorial contests when issues they care about figure prominently in the campaign. Similarly, Christian fundamentalists, although not more likely to vote in Senate elections, are more likely to engage in other acts of political participation in gubernatorial campaigns when the issue of abortion is prominently raised. Moreover, in 1992 liberal women appear to have punished Senate Democrats who supported the Thomas nomination by strategically deciding not to vote at all. All of this suggests that perceptions of issue importance and environmental factors can have powerful effects on rates of political participation.

Alternatively, other groups predisposed to care about abortion and defense issues (i.e., gender and partisan groups) were not more likely to vote when these issues garnered significant attention in Senate campaigns. Also, neither women generally nor women of high socioeconomic status were more likely to participate in politics if abortion was a prominent issue in the selected gubernatorial contests studied in 1998. A complete explanation for these discrepant results is, alas, beyond the scope of this book. I speculate in chapter 7, however, that in addition to high levels of interest and a facilitative political environment, formal organizational ties may also be required to boost levels of political participation (Rosenstone and Hansen 1993). This asset is frequently available to union households and church-going Christian fundamentalists, but not the other groups studied in this book. This account seems plausible, but it does not explain the more positive results uncovered by other researchers. In general, these scholars have found that cues in the political environment can influence participation rates, even among groups without strong organizational ties (Bobo and Gilliam 1990; Hansen 1997; Sapiro and Conover 1997). Much of this literature, however, focuses on the group characteristics of the candidates or incumbent. Perhaps less subtle cues are less effective in the absence of organizational ties. More firm conclusions on this point will have to await future research.

Explaining Democratic Responsiveness

In the first chapter of this book, I briefly outlined four of the main explanations for the relatively high levels of democratic responsiveness in the United States. These are the general partisan or ideological orientation of the district; the ability of the electorate as a whole to cancel out the weaknesses of the individual voter; the mediating role of organized interest groups; and elite attentiveness to, or anticipation of, constituency preferences. Of course, the final model contributed greatly to my own perspective on representation and has been discussed throughout this book. Most of the remaining models were not explicitly tested, but in light of the results summarized above, I can offer some tentative conclusions about which theories work best, and under what circumstances.

District Political Orientation

This theory places particular emphasis on correspondence between the partisan and ideological identifications of constituents and their representative. In my examination of Senate elections, two of the principal control variables were the partisan and ideological correspondence between constituent and senator. These variables, particularly partisan correspondence, were invariably powerful predictors of the vote choice. Similarly, these variables had a significant influence on candidate evaluations in the gubernatorial campaigns studied in chapter 6.

Of course, even after controlling for these measures, I uncovered strong results for perceptions of issue importance. This does not, however, diminish the important roles that partisanship and ideological orientations play in ensuring responsiveness. In fact, even when issues appear to play no role in the vote choice—for example, among Democratic men and Republican women on defense issues (see table 5.2)—they may still exert an influence through their impact on partisanship. Thus the effects uncovered for issue importance do not undermine the role of partisanship so much as they complement it. Lastly, when opportunities for issue voting are limited, as is frequently the case in House elections, then reliance on partisan or ideological cues represent one of the few ways that voters have to select like-minded representatives.

Preference Aggregation

According to this model, aggregate public opinion is more rational and more responsive to the actions of politicians than the individuals making up this collective. This perspective was not directly tested in this book; however, to the extent that my results have implications for this theory, they are decidedly mixed. For example, contrary to the expectations of this model, voters without a particular interest in the issues I examined did not consider their incumbent's performance on these issues when casting their ballots. The one exception to this trend occurred on labor issues. Here I found that even among nonunion households, voters considered their senators' performance on labor issues at election time. This provides some limited support for the idea that the electorate as a whole is not oblivious to their representatives' voting record.

The aggregation process was much more effective when concentrating on the subset of voters most interested in a given issue. This finding does not undermine this model in principle. However, it does suggest that more than just the canceling of random error lends coherence to collective public opinion. As others have also suggested, either those relatively few voters with general interests in political news or citizens with more narrow interests are also required to provide clarity to the "rational public." As indicated above, although this book focuses on the latter, I found evidence for both factors.

Interest Group Pressure

As with the aggregation model, a thorough examination of the interest group model of democratic accountability was beyond the scope of this book. Still, my results also shed some light on this perspective. First, interest groups clearly do play a significant role in transmitting critical political information to its members. Interest group activity helps to explain why union members, and residents in union households, are more politically engaged and active when issues of concern to organized labor are prominent in the political environment. Similarly, the role of interest groups helps to account for the greater attentiveness that Christian fundamentalists had to the anti-abortion platform of California gubernatorial candidate Dan Lungren. Finally, interest groups undoubtedly played a critical role in placing issues such as abortion onto the political agenda in some campaigns for the U.S. Senate.

As illustrated in the Thomas case, however, interest groups are not always the necessary conduits of information. Recall that many African American civil rights organizations either opposed the Thomas nomination or took a neutral position. In either case, these groups surely recognized that their followers adopted a different position. Given this set of circumstances, it is unlikely that these organizations played an important role in publicizing the votes of any particular group of senators. Moreover, given the media attention devoted to this issue, this would probably have been unnecessary. Nevertheless, blacks did learn of their senators' vote on this issue and exerted significant political leverage, all without the aid of intervening interest groups.

Future Research

Two areas of research hold promise as ways of advancing the arguments proposed in this book. The first concerns the unpredictable potential of the Internet. The information environment plays a critical role in facilitating the ability of ordinary citizens to monitor their elected officials. Hence, the Internet represents an important technological innovation that holds enormous promise for the shape of this environment.

Because this medium allows the public unprecedented access to a vast array of information and unique opportunities for political expression, some observers predict a sea change in the workings of our representative democracy (Bimber 1998, 1999; Browning 1996; Hauben and Hauben 1997; Hill and Hughes 1998). For example, civic engagement and political knowledge may grow dramatically as a consequence of the multiple sources of information and communication made possible by the Internet.

An alternative possibility has also been envisioned. Some argue that the rise of the Internet may actually impoverish our democracy (Negroponte 1995; Sunstein 2001). A wider range of news sources, tailored to fit every conceivable viewpoint, might contribute to increased fragmentation and polarization in society. Moreover, voters might simply avoid political information that makes them uncomfortable and eschew any concern with the national interest in favor of their more restrictive views. In some ways, perhaps, this represents a kind of nightmarish perspective on the issue publics hypothesis.

Of course, neither view may come to pass, but the widespread access to, and growing influence of, the Internet calls out for research on its implications for democracy. Future research might concentrate on the ways that individuals use this medium to gather political information, communicate with like-minded citizens and organizations, and contact elected officials. Particular attention should also be focused on the interaction of environmental cues (e.g., campaign communications and news coverage of particular issues) and individual motivation on the political uses of the Internet.

A second way in which future research may enhance our understanding of the process of voter monitoring is through the use of experimental methods. Of course, political scientists have used such methods for some time, particularly with regard to question-wording experiments (Kinder and Sanders 1996; Sniderman and Piazza 1993) and demonstrations of the priming hypothesis (Iyengar and Kinder 1987; Krosnick and Branon 1993; Krosnick and Kinder 1990; Mendelberg 2001). Both trends have advanced our knowledge in a number of important ways, but they also have limited application to the study of democratic accountability. This is because question-wording experiments typically focus on framing issues with the aim of determining how the presentation of an issue resonates with public opinion. Also, as indicated in chapter 1, much of the work on priming has focused on the news media and not the campaign context.

What would be more useful for the questions addressed in this book are experimental studies examining the ways in which differences in the campaign environment (e.g., the absence or presence of particular issues, or the extent to which candidates differ on relevant issues) affect levels of political engagement. Such methods would give us greater confidence than is possible with cross-sectional data in the process by which latent attitudes become activated. Adding experiments to the list of methods employed to learn about voter monitoring would facilitate an examination of presidential contests. At present, such examinations are problematic because national elections are relatively few in number and measuring the local media environment for such contests is difficult.

Conclusion

At the outset of this book, I indicated agreement with the intuition of earlier scholars that the fear of arousing latent public opinion often had the effect of influencing public policy. In order for this fear to remain substantial, however, public opinion must at least occasionally become activated. Previous work in this area has not adequately demonstrated this proposition, nor has anyone detailed the precise circumstance under which the public would become alerted. I believe my emphasis on perceptions of issue importance and elements in the political environment have addressed these shortcomings in the literature. Clearly the public, or perhaps more accurately various issue publics, can become swiftly alerted to political news provided that their motivation is strong and the political context is amenable. Thus, the characterization of the American electorate as a collection of sleeping giants likely to stir if any politician should ignore their interests is not far from the truth.

I do not, however, wish to leave the impression that this particular mechanism of accountability is not without its own share of flaws. Perhaps first among these weaknesses is its heavy reliance on institutional actors such as the media, interest groups, or the major parties to place important issues onto the political agenda. The rise of the Internet may diminish this concern, but, as indicated above, this remains to be seen. For now, it is clear that when the electorate's interests coincide with the institutional interests of these more traditional actors, elites will behave in ways that promote greater accountability. For example, more prominent newspaper coverage of senators who vote against the majority of their party or take active leadership roles serves both the public's and the media's interests. Similarly, political challengers and interest group leaders have a personal stake in identifying instances where the incumbent overlooked the interests of some important segment of the electorate.

Yet, when these interests do not overlap, it becomes easier for politicians to ignore constituent preferences. When the leadership of the Democratic and Republican parties agree on some policy this issue is unlikely to garner much attention from the candidates, even if a significant percentage of the public disagrees with the status quo. A timely example of this might be the manner in which foreign policy is conducted during times of war, or other issues such as international trade agreements, ballot access for third party movements, term limits, or a Canadian-style single-payer system of universal health insurance. In each case, opposition candidates from either of the two major parties are not likely to challenge the status quo. In many cases, interest group opposition will also be muted because the fortunes of most organizations are inextricably tied to the major parties. And, in the absence of overt political conflict, the mass media will also have less interest in raising these issues. As a result, the potential preferences of the electorate are likely to remain dormant.

Finally, an unfortunate implication of this study is that democratic responsiveness merely requires the presence of relatively small, discrete groups that care intensely about particular issues. While there is no shortage of such groups in American society, there are also many important issues that do not easily lend themselves to groups of this type. For example, issues affecting consumers in general, or issues such as campaign finance, do not appeal primarily to a recognizable segment of the electorate. Are politicians less responsive on these issues? It is difficult to provide a definitive answer to this question, although it would seem that such legislation does suffer from the lack of a natural constituency.

In the end, I conclude that public opinion is influential both because of how it *might* respond to elite behavior and, at least occasionally, because of how it *actually* responds. However, much of the influence of these sleeping giants depends on their interests overlapping with those of some elite actor. When this occurs, or when politicians believe this might occur, the likelihood that politicians will diligently reflect the interests of the public is high. When some element of elite interests and the public's interests do not coincide, however, there is little danger that the sleeping giants will stir.

Notes

Chapter 1

1. This argument owes much to the work of John Zaller (1992).

2. The NARAL voting index, along with all other interest group voting indices used in this book, ranges from 0 to 100, with higher values indicating greater support for abortion rights. These indices will be described in greater detail in chapter 5.

3. The relationship between self-interest, group interests, core values, and perceptions of issue importance will be explored in more detail in chapters 3 and 4.

4. The range of policies that groups of citizens perceive as important is far broader than this list of issues implies. In theory, this list should also include attitudes about gun control, business regulation, social security, support for change in elements of the tax code, and a variety of other topics. However, the survey instruments used in this book do not typically ask questions on such a broad range of topics. Moreover, the number of respondents who regard some of these issues as important would likely be too small to be captured by most national surveys. Therefore, the strategy of this book will be to focus only on issues that are deemed important by relatively large subgroups in the electorate. In principle, however, my argument should apply both to issues deemed important by relatively large groups of citizens and to issues of concern to a relative few.

5. In this book, the terms "salience" or "salient" refer to an issue that a group of voters *perceive* to be important, not the objective prominence of the policy in a campaign.

6. For example, examining NES data from 1968, 1980, and 1984, Krosnick (1988) found that issue salience did affect the vote choice. Examining the 1992 Senate elections, however, Wolpert and Gimpel (1997) found that interest in the Thomas hearings did not consistently affect the vote choice.

7. Some recent work has examined the idea of explicit candidate strategies to prime voters. This research typically explains why politicians are drawn to this strategy and why it should affect voters (Jacobs and Shapiro 1994; Mendelberg 2001; Petrocik 1996; Popkin 1991). Still, while this important work has developed a theoretical rationale for candidate priming, it is typically limited by its emphasis on a single campaign.

8. The work of Verba, Burns, and Schlozman (1997), Paolino (1995), and Sapiro and Conover (1997) represent an exception to this rule. Each finds that gender-relevant attitudes have a more powerful effect on political judgments among women voters, especially in contests with female candidates. None of these articles, however, examines other issue domains nor theorizes more generally about the interactions of issue salience and context.

Chapter 2

1. An example of the first might be former Senator Mark Hatfield's lone Republican vote against the Balanced Budget Amendment. An example of the second might be southern Democratic support for the confirmation of Clarence Thomas.

2. The editors of the *Congressional Quarterly Almanac* focus on three criteria in selecting key votes: issues that are a matter of major controversy, issues that are a matter of presidential or political power, and issues that have a potentially significant impact on the nation and the lives of Americans. After determining which issues meet these criteria, the editors then select the specific vote (within each set of important issues) that was most important in determining the outcome.

3. A greater number of key votes were selected, relative to more routine votes. This was done because of an initial interest, later abandoned, in examining both key votes and more "historic" ones (e.g., the Gulf War, Clarence Thomas, and balanced budget votes). Whether or not this distinction is incorporated does not fundamentally alter the conclusions of this chapter.

4. Two were selected for the Senate and two for the House of Representatives.

5. The number of state newspapers sampled varied depending on the year that a particular piece of legislation came up for a vote. This is because some of the online newspapers used in this chapter were unavailable at the time that some bills were voted on. At minimum I examined twenty-two state newspapers (for plant closing legislation) and at most I examined twenty-six. A list of newspapers and their circulation is provided in the appendix to chapter 2.

6. There are certain risks to this approach. Some studies have found that larger papers devote less space than smaller newspapers to members of Congress during their reelection campaigns (Tidmarch, Hyman, and Sorkin 1984).

7. Since about two-thirds of the stories were read via electronic databases (i.e., LexisNexis and Westlaw), it was difficult to determine precisely how much of a front-page story actually appeared on the front page. Consequently, I coded any mention of the member's roll call votes that appeared after the tenth paragraph as falling on the inside of the paper (and thus coded 1). In most cases this seemed a safe assumption, in that it was likely to capture nearly every case in which the reference occurred on the front page. Also, neither LexisNexis nor Westlaw provided information about whether "How They Voted" charts attached to front-page stories appeared on the front page or were inside the paper (where they would be coded 2). My assumption was that the charts did *not* appear on the front page unless there was a clear indication that they did. Admittedly, this may have caused a bias toward underestimating the prominence of roll call reporting. Still, examination of a selection of stories on microfilm indicated that this coding assumption was valid for the vast majority of cases.

8. With few exceptions, newspapers assigned the votes of both senators, or all the House delegation, the same level of coverage. In those few cases where this was not the case (e.g., when the vote of only one senator was reported), the average of the two values was taken.

9. Examining an earlier vote on virtually the same bill in 1991 seems to bear out my suspicions. The median level of coverage for the 1991 bill was 1 for both the Senate and the House. However, a similar number of newspapers (85%) made some mention of how their senators voted on this bill in 1991 as in 1992, whereas considerably fewer (69% in 1991 versus 92% in 1992) did so for the House.

10. Both the Thomas vote and the Carnes vote included one case where the two senators were given different levels of coverage. For example, in the case of the Thomas vote, Ohio Senator Howard Metzenbaum's vote was mentioned in the text of an inside story whereas John Glenn's vote was not mentioned at all. Splitting the difference (1 for Metzenbaum and 0 for Glenn) gives Ohio a score of 0.5. In the case of the Carnes vote, Pennsylvania's Arlen Specter was mentioned in an inside-headline story, whereas Harris Wofford was mentioned only in the text of a (separate) inside story. Thus, Pennsylvania was coded 1.5. For purposes of figure 2.1, these states are both coded up to the closest whole number.

11. Newspaper circulations ranged from 60,086 to 1,169,066. For ease of presentation, this variable was divided by 10,000 so that it now ranges from 6.008 to 116.9.

12. In the case of House members from larger states (e.g., CA, IL, MI, PA, FL, OH, TX, and NY), both the antiparty vote variable and the local connection variable were scored 1 only when referencing a member of the state delegation from the region in which the newspaper circulated. For example, if Rep. Tom Campbell (R-CA) of Northern California voted against his party, this would be coded as a 0 because the newspaper selected for California, the *Los Angeles Times*, is not circulated in his region of the state.

13. Of course, this is not the only way to gauge responsiveness. After all, sometimes when a member of Congress votes with his or her party, this may not reflect the wishes of the constituency. Still, a vote against the party is typically such an unusual act that I think it is an appropriate (albeit rough) measure of exceptional responsiveness or unresponsiveness to constituents.

14. In addition to sponsorship, this variable also included members of Congress who offered important amendments designed to fundamentally alter a particular piece of legislation.

15. This method is necessary because the dependent variable is ordinal and categorical rather than continuous (Greene 1993).

16. These results were obtained by interacting measures of the leadership and party vote variables with the variable measuring whether the vote was routine or key. If the interactions were not statistically significant, they were subsequently excluded from the analysis (see appendix to this chapter).

17. For the striker replacement vote, states where individual members of Congress took an active role in support of, or in opposition to, this roll call were Kansas, where Republican Senator Nancy Kassebaum led efforts to repeal the executive order, and Massachusetts, where Democratic Senator Edward Kennedy led efforts to block the Republicans. For the Carnes nomination, members with an individual connection to the vote included senators from the southern states where the Eleventh Circuit Court had jurisdiction.

18. Clearly, most citizens gain their political information from television and not the print media (Graber 1993). As a result, my decision to focus on newspapers undoubtedly overestimates the attentiveness of the mass media to the voting records of individual legislators. Nevertheless, newspapers are inexpensive and easily accessible. Thus, any citizen who wanted to learn about their representative's vote on a specific piece of legislation could if they chose to do so (assuming the information were made available in the press). In the end, the analyses in

this chapter can only shed light on what citizens could have learned, if sufficiently motivated, rather than what they likely did learn irrespective of their motivation.

19. Graber (1993) notes that for both senators and House members, important institutional leadership positions generate more press coverage than actually taking a leading role in support of or opposition to a specific bill. She writes, "sponsoring legislation or service on important committees matters little. *Who* one is obviously counts more than *what* one does" (294, italics in original). The results of this chapter suggest that this is probably less true for senators than it is for House members.

Chapter 3

1. Self-interest underlies issue importance when "a person perceives an attitude to be instrumental to one's tangible rights, privileges, or lifestyle" (Boninger, Krosnick, and Berent 1995: 63). Identification with a group can lead to perceptions of issue importance when the group's rights or privileges are perceived to be threatened, even though the individual may not be directly affected by this policy. For example, a wealthy African American with strong group identity may vigorously support affirmative action programs even though these policies are unlikely to affect his or her personal situation. Finally, core values are implicated in perceptions of issue importance when public policies invoke beliefs "about how [individuals] ought or ought not to behave, or . . . [when they involve] some end-state of existence worth or not worth attaining" (Rokeach 1968: 124).

2. Judy Wiessler, "Close Vote Favors Thomas: Judge Passes Final Test with 52–48 Senate Tally." *Houston Chronicle*, October 16, 1991, p. A1.

3. Neil A. Lewis, "The Thomas Nomination: Judiciary Panel Deadlocks, 7–7, on Thomas Nomination to Court," *New York Times*, September 27, 1991, p. 1.

4. Ronald Brownstein, "The Times Poll: Public Tends to Believe Thomas by 48% to 35%," *Los Angeles Times*, October 14, 1991, p. A1. Other polls taken at the time arrived at similar results. For example, the *USA Today* found that 63 percent of blacks backed Thomas compared with 55 percent of whites (L. Phillips, "Senators Wary of Political Price: 'Yes' or 'No' Votes Will Cost Support," October 15, 1991, p. 2A).

5. Janet Cawley, Mitchell Locin, and Steve Daley, "Thomas Wins by Narrow Margin: 11 Democrats Provide Votes Bush Needed," *Chicago Tribune*, October 16, 1991, p. C1.

6. Bernie Karsko and Graydon Hambrick, "Local Reaction Mixed on Confirmation," *Columbus Dispatch*, October 16, 1991, p. A2.

7. Aaron Epstein, "Thomas: Time for Healing; Battle Ends with Narrow Victory for Supreme Court Nominee," *Charlotte Observer*, October 16, 1991, p. A1.

8. Ronald Brownstein, "The Times Poll: Public Tends to Believe Thomas by 48% to 35%," *Los Angeles Times*, October 14, 1991, p. A1.

9. Linda Diebel, "Women's Support Key to Thomas," *Toronto Star*, October 17, 1991, p. A18.

10. Richard L. Berke, "Senators Who Switched Tell of Political Torment," *New York Times*, October 16, 1991. The thirteen swing Democrats were senators Boren

(OK), Breaux (LA), Bryan (NV), Dixon (IL), Fowler (GA), Exon (NE), Hollings (SC), Johnston (LA), Lieberman (CT), Nunn (GA), Reid (NV), Robb (VA), and Shelby (AL).

11. Ibid.

12. Lee Bandy, "Hollings: 'Bottom Line Is President's Right to Pick,' " *Charlotte Observer*, October 16, 1991. The *Memphis Commercial Appeal* also reported that "A number of Southern Democrats are up for election next year after narrow victories in 1986 and they noted privately that black voters in their states backed Judge Thomas." James Rowley, "Senate Confirms Thomas, 52–48, to High Court: After Bitter Debate Judge Gets Key Votes of Southern Dems," *Memphis Commercial Appeal*, October 16, 1991.

13. Charles Green and R. A. Zaldivar, "Public Support May Have Been What Put Thomas Over the Top," *New Orleans Time Picayune*, October 16, 1991.

14. The SES survey was also conducted in 1988 and 1990. Responses from these years will be used in subsequent chapters.

15. If respondents indicated that they did not know how their senators voted, they were asked if they would be willing to guess. Those who said they knew and those who were prepared to guess are treated the same in this chapter.

16. Steve Daley and Mitchell Locin, "Day of Reckoning for Thomas: Democrats from South May Hold Key," *Chicago Tribune*, October 15, 1991, p. C1.

17. According to the *Harvard Law Review*, Thomas voted with Antonin Scalia, widely regarded as the most conservative member of the Supreme Court, 85.9 percent of the time in 1991 (Curry and Coleman 1996).

18. These results are based on the ordered logistic regression analyses presented in table 3A in the appendix to this chapter.

19. The probabilities for liberal women are derived from the interaction of ideology and gender (see table 3A). When assessing the significance of an interaction, Jaccard, Turrisi, and Wan (1990) suggest examining how the slope on the interaction term varies as the values of the main effects change. Specifically, they recommend that a coefficient and standard error be calculated for every possible value of the interaction. Using the formula they provide, I find that liberal women are more accurate than conservative women and liberal men, but in the case of liberal men the difference is not statistically significant.

20. An alternative interpretation is that female candidates were more likely to run in states where citizens were already aware and angry about their incumbent's vote. Although this seems a plausible hypothesis, it fails both logically and empirically. Of the eight challengers included in this variable, only two—Lynn Yeakel (PA) and Carol Mosley-Braun (IL)—seem to fit the description. The argument is more of a stretch for the remaining challengers. For example, Dianne Feinstein (CA) declared her intentions to run for the Senate before the Thomas controversy, and Charlene Haar (SD) challenged a Democratic opponent of Thomas. There was no expectation that the other incumbents would oppose Thomas and thus little grounds for anger. Still, if the alternative explanation is true, then the female candidate coefficient should decrease with the exclusion of Pennsylvania and Illinois. Also, attitudes toward Thomas should be more extreme in states with female candidates. Neither assumption is supported by the data.

21. The context and salience measures identified for the Thomas vote are also poor predictors of general levels of political knowledge (Hutchings 2001).

22. Levels of general political information and interest are measured with a series of questions asking respondents to identify the political office held by Tom Foley, Dan Quayle, William Rehnquist, and Al Gore. This scale has five possible values: 0, 0.25, 0.50, 0.75, and 1. Low scores are defined as scores of 0 or 0.25, and high scores are defined as 0.75 or 1.

23. States with female candidates are Arizona, California, Iowa, Kansas, Maryland, Missouri, Pennsylvania, Illinois, and South Dakota. Mosley Braun (D-IL) competed for an open seat in the general election but is also included because she defeated an incumbent in the primary. Barbara Mikulski (D-MD) was the only female incumbent facing reelection.

Chapter 4

1. Carmines and Stimson (1980) define "easy" issues as those that stay on the public agenda for considerable periods of time, require little techical knowledge, and focus more on ends than on means. "Hard" issues, of course, represent a mirror-image of this definition.

2. The SES survey data used to test my hypothesis were described briefly in chapter 3. Here, however, I use responses from 1988 and 1990 in addition to 1992. Overall, the SES included 9,253 respondents, or 3,145, 3,349, and 2,759 in the years 1988, 1990, and 1992, respectively. The actual number of respondents, however, will be reduced by almost half since I focus only on respondents in states with an incumbent facing reelection.

3. As indicated in the appendix, coders were instructed to identify "abortion" as a campaign theme if they encountered any references to it, such as "parental consent restrictions or waiting period(s)" or "public funding of abortions." Labor issues refer to specific references to "the 1988 Plant Closing bill (requiring 60 days' notice before workers could be fired)" and "comments on trade, including references to trade imbalance, import quotas, and exports particularly (but NOT only) when it is implied that Americans might lose jobs because of foreign trade." Included here were also any references to the North American Free Trade Agreement (NAFTA). Defense themes included "references to the Persian Gulf War," "comments about a candidate's failure to serve in the military," "any references to American relations (NONTRADE) with foreign nations," and "discussion of weapons systems."

4. I also tested whether these expectations regarding each issue public and their respective issue were borne out in the SES survey data. Again, there was no question directly measuring respondents' "most important issue," but this survey did include questions on labor issues (e.g., unemployment assistance and limits on foreign imports), defense and foreign affairs (e.g., spending, aid to the Contras, "Star Wars," and attitudes on the Persian Gulf War), and abortion (e.g., support for the policy, as well as parental consent laws and government funding). My aim here was simply to determine if issue public attitudes were *distinctive.* In general I found support for this notion. That is, union membership is a statisti-

cally significant predictor of attitudes on labor issues even after controlling for partisanship, ideology, and standard demographic variables. Similarly, women, Protestant fundamentalists, and Catholics are all significantly more conservative on abortion than are men, even with attitudinal and demographic controls. Moreover, while increasing levels of education are significantly associated with more liberal positions on abortion, the effects are twice as large for women as they are for men. Finally, women are also significantly more liberal than men on defense issues, but the joint effect of gender and partisanship falls short of statistical significance ($p \leq .14$ for a one-tailed test). However, the effects were in the predicted direction.

5. I examined each of the eighty-six campaigns before assigning them to the coders and identified the thirteen most frequently mentioned policy themes. These thirteen issues, along with an option for "other (specify)," were the only options available to the coders.

6. The survey question is worded as follows: "In your state, what issue did the candidates talk about most during the campaign for the Senate?" Up to three responses were recorded.

7. This difference is statistically significant at the .001 level.

8. William J. Eaton, "House Gives Plant-Closing, Trade Bills Big Send-Off," *Louisville Courier-Journal*, July, 14, 1988, p. 1A.

9. I also examined whether high levels of interest in political campaigns, high media usage, or education were also associated with accurately identifying labor issues, but all of these effects were well short of statistical significance and consequently removed from the analysis.

10. Attitudes on this dimension were assessed with a question asking whether respondents supported or opposed increased defense spending.

11. Catholics and fundamentalist Protestants are defined as white respondents who indicated that their religion is Catholic, Baptist, Assembly of God, Church of the Nazarene, Church of Christ, Christian Reformed, Pentecostal, or Orthodox Presbyterian Church (Barker and Carman 1997).

12. High-status respondents are defined as individuals who work outside the home, have four-year college degrees or graduate degrees, and household income of $50,000 or more.

13. The interaction of campaign interest and prominence of the abortion theme actually did achieve borderline statistical significance. However, the substantive effect of the interactive term was negligible and, in any case, in the "wrong" direction. That is, as abortion themes became more prominent, respondents with high levels of general interest in campaigns became mildly less likely to identify this issue.

14. The results in this chapter and the findings of Price and Zaller are not strictly comparable. This is because they measure general political interest with the standard NES information scale, whereas I use either education, news media consumption, or interest in the political campaign. I do not use the information scale because it was available only in the 1992 wave of the SES. However, when the analyses are redone with the 1992 data only, including the information scale has no effect.

Chapter 5

1. They define "class" issues as general labor-consumer issues. Respondents interested in these issues typically made reference to "the cost of living," the Taft-Hartley Law, or "rich man–poor man distinctions in general" (Berelson, Lazarsfeld, and McPhee 1954: 261).

2. Some recent work finds that while the presence of campaigns is important, their specific content has little effect on the election outcome (Bartels 1997; Gelman and King 1993; Markus 1988). Therefore, we cannot be sure that what the Columbia scholars observed in the 1948 election might have occurred regardless of what issues Truman emphasized.

3. As indicated in chapter 4, no labor themes were raised in the 1990 Senate races.

4. See the appendix to this chapter for a fuller description of the model from which the probabilities are derived, as well as the number of cases used to generate the results.

5. This decision was made to simplify the presentation of the results. The substantive impact of the analyses is not significantly altered if we assume different values for the control variables.

6. Labor attitudes are measured with the following question: "Should federal spending on government assistance for the unemployed be increased, decreased, or kept about the same?"

7. Moderate levels of prominence are defined as campaigns in which the probability of learning of a theme are .5. High levels of prominence are defined as campaigns where the probability of learning of the issue is all but certain at 1.00.

8. These results are statistically significant, as shown in the second column of table 5A.

9. This effect achieves borderline statistical significance in the full model ($p \leq .10$; see appendix to this chapter). However, given the number of interactions in the model, it is likely that this is due to the relatively high level of colinearity. When the nonsignificant higher-order interactions are removed from the model, the COPE score × labor attitude interaction becomes more significant ($p \leq .05$).

10. There is considerable variance among both Senate Democrats and Republicans on the NSI index. For example, Senator Kennedy of Massachusetts scored 0 on the NSI index in 1988 and Senator Nunn of Georgia scored 100 in 1990. Among Republicans, Senator Hatfield of Oregon scored 10 on this index in 1988, whereas many other senators in his party scored at or near 100.

11. This table probably understates the political significance of abortion, in part because partisan identification is held constant. As Adams (1997) and others have argued, some citizens have altered their partisan identification in large part because of this issue.

12. With the exception of the National Security Index, which comes out every two years, each of these interest groups publishes annual ratings on members of Congress. For purposes of consistency, the COPE and NARAL ratings were averaged over a full two-year session of Congress. All of the interest group ratings were modified so that missing votes did not count against legislators.

13. The party disagreement variable was constructed such that it was equal to 0 when the respondent and the incumbent belonged to the same party, 1 if the

respondent was an independent, and 2 if there was disagreement. Strong and weak party identifiers as well as independent "leaners" are all collapsed into a single category with only true independents classified as neutral. The ideological disagreement variable was constructed by subtracting the respondents' placement of themselves on the 7-point ideological scale from the *average value* their senators were given in each state and then taking the absolute value. The campaign competitiveness variable was taken from assessments from *Congressional Quarterly's Weekly Report*. Finally, the incumbent's partisanship was interacted with presidential approval on the premise that respondents who liked the president would also like Senate incumbents belonging to the same party.

Chapter 6

1. According to Barone and Ujifusa (1999), Ryan's "October ads hit Poshard as too conservative and 'extreme, extreme, extreme.' " Chicago area liberals also criticized Poshard for his positions on gun control and gay rights, and his opposition to the Clean Air Act.

2. This battery of questions was introduced with the following introduction: "We are interested in what candidates are talking about in their campaigns. For each issue we would like to know if you think either one of the candidates, both, or neither is talking about these issues." The respondents were then asked about a series of issues, including "protecting a woman's right to an abortion." This phrase may unfortunately imply to some respondents that the candidate also *supported* a woman's right to an abortion. If so, then pro-life candidates who spent considerable time discussing the issue might erroneously be characterized as not talking about abortion. This problem appears not to have been too serious, however, as the pro-life candidate who focused on this issue the most—California Republican Dan Lungren—was also perceived by respondents as emphasizing this issue more than any other pro-life candidate.

3. This variable is defined somewhat differently from the definition in chapters 4 and 5. In those chapters, Christian fundamentalists were defined simply by their religious affiliation. Unlike the SES data, however, the pilot-study data contain items asking respondents if they consider themselves members of fundamentalist, evangelical, or charismatic religious groups. Additionally, respondents were asked how frequently they attend church services. Respondents identifying themselves as members of these religious groups and who also indicated that they attend church every week, or almost every week, were classified as "fundamentalists."

4. In chapters 4 and 5, these were defined as college-educated respondents who earned high incomes and worked outside of the home. To preserve an adequate number of cases for analysis, we focus only on college graduates in this chapter.

5. See table 6A in the appendix to this chapter for the logistic regression analyses from which these figures are drawn.

6. Interestingly, these effects are not enhanced among fundamentalists with high levels of general political knowledge. In fact, the reverse is true: the higher fundamentalists score on the general information scale, the *less* likely they are to indicate that Lungren discussed abortion during the campaign. Part of the explanation for this is that fundamentalists who score low on the information

scale are also more likely to attend church "weekly or more often." Presumably, then, they learned of Lungren's pro-life message because of their organizational affiliation as well as the importance they attach to the issue of abortion.

7. The figures in the fourth column of table 6.3 are based only on those respondents who answered at least two of the political information questions correctly (55%). The political information scale consisted of questions on which branch of government decides if a law is constitutional, which branch nominates judges to the federal courts, which party controls the House of Representatives, and which party has the most members in the U.S. Senate.

8. Only the perception of which candidate would best represent a group and issue importance is varied in figures 6.4 through 6.6. All other variables are held constant. For example, the partisanship of respondents is assumed to be Independent, and their ideology is assumed to be moderate. All other variables are held at their mean or median.

9. Only 45 out of the 348 California respondents who indicated that they were likely to vote in November viewed the Republican candidate as the better representative of labor unions. In contrast, 197 respondents, including most Republicans, perceived the Democratic candidate as more likely to effectively represent this group's interests.

10. Given the stated positions of the candidates in California, these results may also represent a kind of "projection" effect (Franklin 1991; Page and Brody 1972). In other words, respondents who backed Lungren may have also concluded that he would effectively represent this group rather than first deciding that he would do better for the group and consequently deciding to support him.

11. The California sample included 400 respondents, whereas the Georgia and Illinois samples included 401 and 402 respondents, respectively.

12. The order in which the Democratic and Republican candidates were presented in the question was randomized across respondents. Respondents were also asked about "conservative religious groups such as the Christian Coalition" and "environmental protection groups such as the Sierra Club." These groups are not included in the analyses in this chapter because the former group's interests overlap considerably with prolife groups, and the survey questions do not allow for an obvious way of identifying those most concerned about the latter group.

13. There were two versions of this question in the pilot study. Half of the sample was simply asked if they would vote "this coming November/next week." The other half was asked to rate the probability that they would vote. Those respondents who provided an answer other than "yes" in the first half-sample were dropped from the analysis, as were those indicating that the probability was less than .50. Only about 15 percent of respondents indicated that they probably would not vote.

Chapter 7

1. A single, albeit high-profile, vote is more likely to affect a voters' political decision if he or she is on the losing side of an issue (Arnold 1990; Fenno 1989). As indicated in chapter 3, conservative men and African Americans were also

especially attentive to the Thomas vote. However, in the end these groups achieved the result that they preferred with Thomas's successful confirmation.

2. Fenno (1996) provides some support for this hypothesis in his book *Senators on the Campaign Trail.* He notes that Senator Fowler (D-GA), one of the swing Democrats up for reelection in 1992, encountered a considerable lack of enthusiasm among liberal women because of his vote. "[Fowler's] single most harmful failure to keep in touch involved his inattentiveness to a core element of his 1986 coalition—the strongly supportive liberal, pro-choice women who had become disaffected in the wake of his vote in support of conservative, anti-abortion Clarence Thomas for the Supreme Court" (1996: 194).

3. Results were also examined among liberal and conservative men. As anticipated, no clear pattern emerged in these analyses.

4. For example, a 2 on the item measuring a respondent's efforts to persuade someone how to vote indicated that he or she tried at least three times to persuade someone.

5. According to the 1988–1992 SES, almost 9 percent of California residents belonged to a labor union versus about 11 percent of Illinois residents.

6. The two states also differed in terms of the competitiveness of the Democratic primaries. In California, Gray Davis faced two serious challengers early on but in the end wound up with an impressive 58 percent of the vote. In Illinois, Glenn Poshard faced two tough primary opponents and managed to win with only 38 percent of the vote. Poshard was also strongly backed by organized labor in the primary, and it is possible that the participation rates of union households are linked to this contest and not the general election.

References

Abramowitz, Alan I. 1988. "Explaining Senate Election Outcomes." *American Political Science Review* 82:385–403.

———. 1995. "It's Abortion Stupid: Policy Voting in the 1992 Presidential Election." *Journal of Politics* 57:176–86.

Adams, Greg D. 1997. "Abortion: Evidence of Issue Evolution." *American Journal of Political Science* 41(3):718–37.

Aldrich, John H., John L. Sullivan, and Eugene Borgida. 1989. "Foreign Affairs and Issue Voting: Do Presidential Candidates 'Waltz Before a Blind Audience'?" *American Political Science Review* 83:123–41.

Althaus, Scott L. 1998. "Information Effects in Collective Preferences." *American Political Science Review* 92(2):545–58.

Alvarez, R. Michael. 1997. *Information and Elections.* Ann Arbor: University of Michigan Press.

Alvarez, R. Michael, and Paul Gronke. 1996. "Constituents and Knowledge of Senate Roll Call Votes." Presented at the American Political Science Association.

Ansolabehere, Stephen, Roy Behr, and Shanto Iyengar. 1993. *The Media Game.* New York: Macmillan.

Arnold, R. Douglas. 1990. *The Logic of Congressional Action.* New Haven: Yale University Press.

Barker, David C., and Christopher Jan Carman. 1997. "Fundamentalist Religiosity and Ideological Constraint." Presented at the Midwest Political Science Association.

Barone, Michael, and Grant Ujifusa. 1993. *The Almanac of American Politics 1994.* Washington, DC: National Journal.

———. 1999. *The Almanac of American Politics 2000.* Washington, D.C.: National Journal.

Bartels, Larry M. 1991. "Constituency Opinion and Congressional Policy Making: The Reagan Defense Buildup." *American Political Science Review* 85:457–72.

———. 1992. "The Impact of Electioneering in the United States." In *Electioneering: A Comparative Study of Continuity and Change,* ed. David Butler and Austin Ranney. Oxford: Clarendon Press.

———. 1996. "Uninformed Votes: Information Effects in Presidential Elections." *American Journal of Political Science* 40(1):194–230.

———. 1997. "How Campaigns Matter." Princeton University. Ms.

Bennett, Stephen Earl. 1995. "Comparing Americans' Political Information in 1988 and 1992." *Journal of Politics* 57:521–32.

Berelson, Bernard, Paul Lazarsfeld, and William McPhee. 1954. *Voting.* New York: Free Press.

Bimber, B. 1998. "The Internet and Political Transformation: Populism, Community and Accelerated Pluralism." *Polity* 31:133–60.

————. 1999. "The Internet and Citizen Communication with Government: Does the Medium Matter?" *Political Communication* 16:409–28.

Blumer, Herbert. 1948. "Public Opinion and Public Opinion Polling." *American Sociological Review* 13:542–54.

Bobo, Lawrence, and Franklin D. Gilliam Jr. 1990. "Race, Sociopolitical Participation, and Black Empowerment." *American Political Science Review* 84:377–93.

Boninger, David S., Jon A. Krosnick, and Matthew K. Berent. 1995. "Origins of Attitude Importance: Self-Interest, Social Identification, and Value Relevance." *Journal of Personality and Social Psychology* 68:61–80.

Browning, G. 1996. *Electronic Democracy: Using the Internet to Influence American Politics.* Wilton, CT: Pemberton Press.

Burnham, Margaret A. 1992. "The Supreme Court Appointment Process and the Politics of Race and Sex." In *Race-ing Justice, En-Gendering Power*, ed. Toni Morrison. New York: Pantheon Books.

Burns, Nancy, Kay Lehman Schlozman, and Sidney Verba. 1997. "The Public Consequences of Private Inequality: Family Life and Citizen Participation." *American Political Science Review* 91:373–89.

Caldeira, Gregory A., and Charles E. Smith, Jr. 1996. "Campaigning for the Supreme Court: The Dynamics of Public Opinion on the Thomas Nomination." *Journal of Politics* 58:655–81.

Campbell, Andrea. 2003. *How Policies Make Citizens: Senior Citizen Activism and the American Welfare State.* Princeton: Princeton University Press.

Campbell, Angus, Phillip E. Converse, Warren E. Miller, and Donald E. Stokes. 1960. *The American Voter.* New York: Wiley.

Carmines, Edward G., and James A. Stimson. 1980. "The Two Faces of Issue Voting." *American Political Science Review* 74:78–91.

————. 1989. *Issue Evolution: Race and the Transformation of American Politics.* Princeton: Princeton University Press.

Chaffee, Steven H., and Donna G. Wilson. 1977. "Media Rich, Media Poor: Two Studies of Diversity in Agenda Holding." *Journalism Quarterly* 54:466–76.

Condorcet, Marie-Jean-Antoine-Nicolas de Caritat, Marquis de. [1785] 1976. Essai sur l'application de l'analyse a la probabilité des decisions rendues à la pluralité des voix. In *Condorcet: Selected Writings*, ed. Keith Michael Baker. Indianapolis: Bobbs-Merrill.

Conover, Pamela Johnston. 1981. "Political Cues and the Perception of Candidates." *American Politics Quarterly* 9:427–48.

————. 1984. "The Influence of Group Identifications on Political Perception and Evaluation." *Journal of Politics* 46:760–84.

————. 1985. "The Impact of Group Economic Interests on Political Evaluations." *American Politics Quarterly* 13:139–66.

————. 1988. "The Role of Social Groups in Political Thinking." *British Journal of Political Science* 18:51–76.

Conover, Pamela Johnston, and Stanley Feldman. 1981. "The Origins and Meanings of Liberal/Conservative Self Identification." *American Journal of Political Science* 25:617–45.

Converse, Philip E. 1964. "The Nature of Belief Systems in Mass Publics." In *Ideology and Discontent*, ed. David Apter. New York: Free Press.

———. 1975. "Public Opinion and Voting Behavior." in *Handbook of Political Science*, vol. 4, ed. F. I. Greenstein and N. W. Polsby. Boston: Addison -Wesley.

———. 1990. "Popular Representation and the Distribution of Information." In *Information and Democratic Processes*, ed. J. Ferejohn and J. Kuklinski. Urbana: University of Illinois Press.

Converse, Philip E., and Gregory Markus. 1979. " 'Plus ça Change. . .': The New CPS Election Study Panel." *American Political Science Review* 73:32–49.

Cook, Elizabeth A., Ted G. Jelen, and Clyde Wilcox. 1992. *Between Two Absolutes: Public Opinion and the Politics of Abortion.* Boulder: Westview Press.

———. 1994. "Issue Voting in Gubernatorial Elections: Abortion and Post-Webster Politics." *Journal of Politics* 56:187–99.

Cook, Elizabeth, Sue Thomas, and Clyde Wilcox. 1994. *The Year of the Woman.* Boulder: Westview Press.

Cook, Timothy E. 1989. *Making Laws and Making News.* Washington, D.C.: Brookings Institution.

Curry, George E., and Trevor W. Coleman. 1996. "The Verdict on Judge Thomas." *Emerge* 8(2): 38–48.

Dahl, Robert A. 1989. *Democracy and Its Critics.* New Haven: Yale University Press.

Dalager, Jon K. 1996. "Voters, Issues, and Elections: Are the Candidates' Messages Getting Through?" *Journal of Politics* 58:486–515.

Davidson, Roger and Walter Oleszek. 1998. *Congress and Its Members.* Washington D. C.: Congressional Quarterly Press.

Dawson, Michael C. 1994. *Behind the Mule: Race and Class in African-American Politics.* Princeton: Princeton University Press.

Day, Christine L. 1990. *What Older Americans Think.* Princeton: Princeton University Press.

———. 1993. "Older Americans' Attitude toward the Medicare Catastrophic Coverage Act of 1988." *Journal of Politics* 55:167–77.

Delli Carpini, Michael X., and Scott Keeter. 1996. *What Americans Know about Politics and Why It Matters.* New Haven: Yale University Press.

Downs, Anthony. 1957. *An Economic Theory of Democracy.* New York: Harper and Row.

Eaton, William J. 1988. "House Gives Plant-Closing, Trade Bills Big Send-Off." *Louisville Courier-Journal,* July 14, A.

Epstein, Aaron. 1991. "Thomas: Time for Healing.' Battle Ends with Narrow Victory for Supreme Court Nominee." *Charlotte Observer,* Oct. 16, A1.

Erbring, Lutz, Edie N. Goldenberg, and Arthur H. Miller. 1980. "Front-Page News and Real-World Cues: A New Look at Agenda Setting by the Media." *American Journal of Political Science* 24:16–49.

Erikson, Robert S. 1978. "Constituency Opinion and Congressional Behavior: A Reexamination of the Miller-Stokes Representation Data." *American Journal of Political Science* 22:511–35.

Erikson, Robert S., and Norman R. Luttbeg. 1973. *American Public Opinion: Its Origins, Content, and Impact.* New York: Wiley.

Erikson, Robert S., and Gerald C. Wright. 1989. "Voters, Candidates, and Issues in Congressional Elections." In *Congress Reconsidered,* ed. Lawrence C. Dodd and Bruce I. Oppenheimer. Washington, DC: Congressional Quarterly.

Fenno, Richard. 1978. *Home Style: House Members in Their Districts.* New York: HarperCollins.

———. 1996. *Senators on the Campaign Trail: The Politics of Representation.* Norman: University of Oklahoma Press.

Finkel, Steven E. 1993. "Reexamining the 'Minimal Effects' Model in Recent Presidential Campaigns." *Journal of Politics* 55:1–21.

Fiorina, Morris P. 1974. *Representatives, Roll Calls, and Constituencies.* Lexington, MA: D.C. Heath.

———. 1981. *Retrospective Voting in American National Elections.* New Haven: Yale University Press.

Fiske, Susan T., and Shelly E. Taylor. 1991. *Social Cognition.* 2d ed. New York: McGraw-Hill.

Franklin, Charles H. 1984. "Issue Preferences, Socialization and the Evolution of Party Identification." *American Journal of Political Science* 28:459–78.

———. 1991. "Eschewing Obfuscation? Campaigns and the Perception of U.S. Senate Incumbents." *American Political Science Review* 85:1193–1214.

Gelman, Andrew, and Gary King. 1993. "Why Are American Presidential Election Campaign Polls So Variable When Votes Are So Predictable?" *British Journal of Political Science* 23:409–51.

Goldenberg, Edie N., and Michael W. Traugott. 1987. "Mass Media Effects on Recognizing and Rating Candidates in U.S. Senate Elections." In *Campaigns in the News: Mass Media and Congressional Elections,* ed. Jan P. Vermeer. New York: Greenwood Press.

Graber, Doris A. 1993. *Mass Media and American Politics.* Washington, DC: Congressional Quarterly Press.

Greene, William H. 1993. *Econometric Analysis.* 2d ed: New York: Macmillan.

Grofman, Benard, and Barbara Norrander. 1990. "Efficient Use of Reference Group Cues in a Single Dimension." *Public Choice* 64:213–27.

Gurin, Patricia. 1985. "Women's Changing Roles." *Public Opinion Quarterly* 49:143–63.

Hall, Richard, and Frank Wayman. 1990. "Buying Time: Moneyed Interests and the Mobilization of Bias in Congressional Committees." *American Political Science Review* 84(3):797–820.

Hamilton, Alexander, James Madison, and John Jay. 1961. *The Federalist Papers.* New York: New American Library.

Hansen, Susan B. 1997. "Talking about Politics: Gender and Contextual Effects on Political Proselytizing." *Journal of Politics* 59:73–103.

Hauben, M. and R. Hauben 1997. *Netizens: On the History and Impact of Usenet and the Internet.* Los Alamitos, CA: IEEE Computer Society Press.

Hill, K. A., and J. E. Hughes. 1998. *Cyberpolitics: Citizen Activism in the Age of the Internet.* Lanham, MD: Rowman and Littlefield.

Huckfeldt, Robert. 1986. *Politics in Context: Assimilation and Conflict in Urban Neighborhoods.* New York: Agathon Press.

Huckfeldt, Robert, and John Sprague. 1995. *Citizens, Politics, and Social Communication: Information and Influence in an Election Campaign.* Cambridge: Cambridge University Press.

Hutchings, Vincent L. 1998. "Issue Salience and Support for Civil Rights Legislation among Southern Democrats." *Legislative Studies Quarterly* 23(4):521–44.

———. 2001. "Political Context, Issue Salience, and Selective Attentiveness: Constituent Knowledge of the Clarence Thomas Confirmation Vote." *Journal of Politics* 63(3):846–68.

Hutchings, Vincent L., Harwood McClerking, and Guy-Uriel Charles. 2000. "When Does Race Matter for Congressional Responsiveness? An Examination of Support for Black Interests in the 101st through 103rd Congress." Presented at the National Conference of Black Political Scientists, Washington, DC.

Hutchings, Vincent L., Nicholas A. Valentino, Tasha S. Philpot, and Ismail White. 2001. "Compassionate Conservatism or Drive-by Photo Opportunity? Candidate Distance, Group Threat, and Campaign Communications." Presented at the American Political Science Association, San Francisco.

Iyengar, Shanto. 1990. "Shortcuts to Political Knowledge: The Role of Selective Attention and Accessibility." In *Information and Democratic Processes*, ed. J. Ferejohn and J. Kuklinski. Urbana: University of Illinois Press.

Iyengar, Shanto, and Donald R. Kinder. 1987. *News That Matters*. Chicago: University of Chicago Press.

Jaccard, James, Robert Turrisi, and Choi K. Wan. 1990. *Interaction Effects in Multiple Regression*. Newbury Park: Sage Publications.

Jackson, John E., and David C. King. 1989. "Public Goods, Private Interests, and Representation." *American Political Science Review* 83:1193–64.

Jacobs, Lawrence R., and Robert Y. Shapiro. 1994. "Issues, Candidate Images, and Priming: The Use of Private Polls in Kennedy's 1960 Presidential Campaign." *American Political Science Review* 88:527–40.

Jacobson, Gary C. 1989. "Strategic Politicians and the Dynamics of U.S. House Elections, 1946–1986." *American Political Science Review* 83:775–93.

———. 1992. *The Politics of Congressional Elections*. New York: HarperCollins.

Jacobson, Gary C., and Samuel Kernell, 1981. *Strategy and Choice in Congressional Elections*. New Haven: Yale University Press.

Jennings, M. Kent. 1992. "Ideology among Mass Publics and Political Elites." *Public Opinion Quarterly* 56:419–41.

Kahn, Kim Fridkin. 1991. "Senate Elections in the News: Examining Campaign Coverage." *Legislative Studies Quarterly* 16:349–76.

———. 1995. "Characteristics of Press Coverage in Senate and Gubernatorial Elections: Information Available to Voters." *Legislative Studies Quarterly* 20:23–35.

Kahn, Kim Fridkin, and Patrick J. Kenny. 1999. *The Spectacle of U.S. Senate Campaigns*. Princeton: Princeton University Press.

Key, V.O. 1961. *Public Opinion and American Democracy*. New York: Knopf.

———. 1966. *The Responsible Electorate: Rationality in Presidential Voting, 1936–1960*. Cambridge: Harvard University Press.

Kinder, Donald R., and Roderick D. Kiewiet. 1981. "Sociotropic Politics." *British Journal of Political Science* 11:129–61.

Kinder, Donald R., and Lynn Sanders. 1996. *Divided by Color: Racial Politics and Democratic Ideals*. Chicago: University of Chicago Press.

Kingdon, John W. 1989. *Congressmen's Voting Decisions.* 3d ed. New York: Harper and Row.

Kingdon, John W., and John E. Jackson. 1992. "Ideology, Interest Group Scores, and Legislative Votes." *American Journal of Political Science* 36:805-23.

Knight, Kathleen. 1985. "Ideology in the 1980 Election: Ideological Sophistication Does Matter." *Journal of Politics* 47:828–53.

———. 1990. "Ideology and Public Opinion." *Micropolitics* 3:59–82.

Kollman, Ken. 1998. *Outside Lobbying: Public Opinion and Interest Group Strategies.* Princeton: Princeton University Press.

Krosnick, Jon A. 1988. "The Role of Attitude Importance in Social Evaluation: A Study of Policy Preferences, Presidential Candidate Evaluations, and Voting Behavior." *Journal of Personality and Social Psychology* 55:240–55.

———. 1990a. "Expertise and Political Psychology." *Social Cognition* 8:1–8.

———. 1990b. "Government Policy and Citizen Passion: A Study of Issue Publics in Contemporary America." *Political Behavior* 12:59–92.

———. 1993. "The Impact of the Gulf War on the Ingredients of Presidential Evaluations: Multidimensional Effects of Political Involvement." *American Political Science Review* 87:963–75.

Krosnick, Jon A., Matthew K. Berent, and David S. Boninger. 1994. "Pockets of Responsibility in the American Electorate: Findings of a Research Program on Attitude Importance." *Political Communication* 11:391–411.

Krosnick, Jon A., and Laura Brannon. 1993. "The Impact of the Gulf War on the Ingredients of Presidential Evaluations: Multidimensional Effects of Political Involvement." *American Political Science Review* 87:963–78.

Krosnick, Jon A., and Donald R. Kinder. 1990. "Altering the Foundations of Support for the President through Priming." *American Political Science Review* 84:497–512.

Kuklinski, James H., Michael D. Cobb, and Martin Gilens. 1997. "Racial Attitudes and the 'New South.'" *Journal of Politics* 59:323–49.

Lau, Richard R., Thad A. Brown, and David O. Sears. 1978. "Self-Interest and Civilians' Attitudes toward the Vietnam War." *Public Opinion Quarterly* 42(4): 464–83.

Lau, Richard R., and David O. Sears, eds. 1986. *Political Cognition: The 19th Annual Carnegie Symposium on Cognition.* Hillsdale, NJ.: Lawrence Erlbaum.

Lazarsfeld, Paul, Bernard Berelson, and Helen Gaudet. 1944. *The People's Choice.* New York: Duell, Sloane, and Pearce.

Lipset, Seymour Martin. [1959] 1981. *Political Man: The Social Bases of Politics.* Baltimore: The Johns Hopkins University Press.

Lodge, Milton, Kathleen M. McGraw, and Patrick Stroh. 1989. "An Impression-Driven Model of Candidate Evaluation." *American Political Science Review* 83:399–419.

Lodge, Milton, Marco R. Steenbergen, and Shawn Brau. 1995. "The Responsive Voter: Campaign Information and the Dynamics of Candidate Evaluation." *American Political Science Review* 89:309–26.

Lublin, David. 1997. *The Paradox of Representation: Racial Gerrymandering and Minority Interests in Congress.* Princeton: Princeton University Press.

Luker, Kristin. 1984. *Abortion and the Politics of Motherhood.* Berkeley and Los Angeles: University of California Press.

Lupia, Arthur. 1994. "Shortcuts versus Encyclopedias: Information and Voting Behavior in California Insurance Reform Elections." *American Political Science Review* 88:63–76.

Lupia, Arthur, and Matthew D. McCubbins. 1998. *The Democratic Dilemma: Can Citizens Learn What They Need to Know?* Cambridge: Cambridge University Press.

Luskin, Robert C. 1990. "Explaining Political Sophistication." *Political Behavior* 12:331–61.

McGraw, Kathleen M., and Neil Pinney. 1990. "The Effects of General and Domain-Specific Expertise on Political Memory and Judgement." *Social Cognition* 8:9–30.

McKelvey, Richard D., and Peter C. Ordeshook. 1990. "Information and Elections: Retrospective Voting and Rational Expectations." In *Information and Democratic Processes,* ed. J. Ferejohn and J. Kuklinski. Urbana: University of Illinois Press.

Mann, Thomas E., and Raymond E. Wolfinger. 1980. "Candidates and Parties in Congressional Elections." *American Political Science Review* 74:617–32.

Mansbridge, Jane, and Katherine Tate. 1992. "Race Trumps Gender: The Thomas Nomination in the Black Community." *PS: Political Science and Politics* 25:488–92.

Marable, Manning. 1992. "Clarence Thomas and the Crisis of Black Political Culture." In *Race-ing Justice, En-Gendering Power,* ed. Toni Morrison. New York: Pantheon Books.

Marcus, George E., and Michael B. MacKuen. 1993. "Anxiety, Enthusiasm, and the Vote: The Emotional Underpinnings of Learning and Involvement during Presidential Campaigns." *American Political Science Review* 87:672–85.

Margolis, Michael. 1977. "From Confusion to Confusion: Issues and the American Voter (1956–1972)." *American Political Science Review* 71:31–43.

Markus, Gregory B. 1988. "The Impact of Personal and National Economic Conditions on the Presidential Vote: A Pooled Cross-Sectional Analysis." *American Journal of Political Science* 32(1):137-54.

Mayhew, David R. 1974. *Congress: The Electoral Connection.* New Haven: Yale University Press.

Mendelberg, Tali. 2001. *The Race Card: Campaign Strategy, Implicit Messages, and the Norm of Equality.* Princeton: Princeton University Press.

Miller, Warren E., and Donald E. Stokes. 1963. "Constituency Influence in Congress." *American Political Science Review* 57(1):45–57.

Mueller, John E. 1994. Policy and Opinion in the Gulf War. Chicago: University of Chicago Press.

Negroponte N. 1995. *Being Digital.* New York: Knopf.

Nie, Norman, Jane Junn, and Kenneth Stehlik-Barry. 1996. *Education and Democratic Citizenship in America.* Chicago: University of Chicago Press.

Nie, Norman, Sidney Verba, and John R. Petrocik. 1976. *The Changing American Voter.* Cambridge: Harvard University Press.

Niemi, Richard G., and Larry M. Bartels. 1985. "New Measures of Issue Salience: An Evaluation." *Journal of Politics* 47:1221–30.

Niemi, Richard G., and Herbvert F. Weisberg. 1993. *Controversies in Voting Behavior.* 3d ed. Washington, DC: Congressional Quarterly Press.

Nueman, W. Russell. 1986. *The Paradox of Mass Politics: Knowledge and Opinion in the American Electorate.* Cambridge: Harvard University Press.

Nye, Mary Alice, and Charles S. Bullock III. 1992. "Civil Rights Support: A Comparison of Southern and Border State Representatives." *Legislative Studies Quarterly* 17:81–94.

Overby, L. Marvin, Beth M. Henschen, Michael H. Walsh, and Julie Strauss. 1992. "Courting Constituents? An Analysis of the Senate Confirmation Vote on Justice Clarence Thomas." *American Political Science Review* 86:997–1003.

Page, Benjamin I. 1978. *Choices and Echoes in Presidential Elections: Rational Man and Electoral Democracy.* Chicago: University of Chicago Press.

Page, Benjamin I., and Richard A. Brody. 1972. "Policy Voting and the Electoral Process: The Vietnam War Issue." *American Political Science Review* 66(3): 979–95.

Page, Benjamin I., and Robert Y. Shapiro. 1992. *The Rational Public.* Chicago: University of Chicago Press.

Paolino, Phillip. 1995. "Group Salient Issues and Group Representation: Support for Women Candidates in the 1992 Senate Elections." *American Journal of Political Science* 39:294–313.

Patterson, Thomas E. 1994. *Out of Order.* New York: Vintage Books.

Patterson, Thomas, and Robert McClure. 1976. *The Unseeing Eye: The Myth of Television Power in National Politics.* New York: Putnam.

Petrocik, John R. 1987. "Realignment: New Party Coalitions and the Nationalization of the South." *Journal of Politics* 49:347–75.

———. 1996. "Issue Ownership in Presidential Elections, with a 1980 Case Study." *American Journal of Political Science* 40:825–50.

Pinderhughes, Dianne M. 1992. "Divisions in the Civil Rights Community." *PS: Political Science and Politics* 25:485–87.

Pomper, Gerald M. 1972. "From Confusion to Clarity: Issues and American Voters, 1956–1968." *American Political Science Review* 66:415–28.

Popkin, Samuel L. 1991. *The Reasoning Voter: Communication and Persuasion in Presidential Campaigns.* Chicago: University of Chicago Press.

Popkin, Samuel L., J. W. Gorman, C. Phillips, and J. A. Smith. 1976. "What Have You Done for Me Lately? Toward an Investment Theory of Voting." *American Political Science Review* 70:779–805.

Powell, Lynda W. 1982. "Issue Representation in Congress." *Journal of Politics* 44:658–78.

Price, Vincent, and John Zaller. 1993. "Who Gets the News?" *Public Opinion Quarterly* 57(2):133–64.

Rabinowitz, George, and Stuart Elaine Macdonald. 1989. "A Directional Theory of Issue Voting." *American Political Science Review* 83:93-121.

Rabinowitz, George, James W. Prothro, and William Jacoby. 1982. "Salience as a Factor in the Impact of Issues on Candidate Evaluation." *Journal of Politics* 44:41–63.

Repass, David E. 1971. "Issue Salience and Party Choice." *American Political Science Review* 65:389–400.

Rokeach, M. 1968. *Beliefs, Attitudes, and Values.* San Francisco: Josey-Bass.

————. 1973. *The Nature of Human Values*. New York: Free Press.

Rosenstone, Steven J., and John Mark Hansen. 1993. *Mobilization, Participation, and Democracy in America*. New York: Macmillan.

Sapiro, Virginia, and Pamela Johnston Conover. 1997. "The Variable Gender Basis of Electoral Politics: Gender and Context in the 1992 U.S. Election." *British Journal of Political Science* 27:497–523.

Schuman, Howard, Charlotte G. Steeh, and Lawrence Bobo. 1985. *Racial Attitudes in American: Trends and Interpretations*. Cambridge: Harvard University Press.

Scott, Jacqueline, and Howard Schuman. 1988. "Attitude Strength and Social Action in the Abortion Dispute." *American Sociological Review* 53(5):785–93.

Sears, David O., and J. L. Freedman. 1967. "Selective Exposure to Information: A Critical Review." *Public Opinion Quarterly* 31:194–213.

Shapiro, Catherine R., David W. Brady, Richard A. Brody, and John Ferejohn. 1990. "Linking Consituency Opinion and Senate Voting Scores: A Hybrid Explanation." *Legislative Studies Quarterly* 15:599–621.

Shapiro, Robert Y., and Harpreet Mahajan. 1986. "Gender Differences in Policy Preferences: A Summary of Trends from the 1960's to the 1980's." *Public Opinion Quarterly* 50:42–61.

Smith, Eric R.A.N. 1989. *The Unchanging American Voter*. Berkeley: University of California Press.

Smith, Robert C. 1996. *We Have No Leaders: African Americans in the Post–Civil Rights Era*. Albany: State University of New York Press.

Smith, Tom W. 1984. "The Polls: Gender and Attitudes about Violence." *Public Opinion Quarterly* 48:384–96.

Sniderman, Paul M., and Thomas Piazza. 1993. *The Scar of Race*. Cambridge: Harvard University Press.

Squire, Peverill, and Christina Fastnow. 1994. "Comparing Gubernatorial and Senatorial Elections." *Political Research Quarterly* 47:705–20.

Stokes, Donald E., and Warren E. Miller. 1962. "Party Government and the Saliency of Congress." *Public Opinion Quarterly* 77:945–56.

Sullivan, J. L., J. E. Piereson, and G. E. Marcus. 1979. "An Alternative Conceptualization of Political Tolerance: Illusory Increases, 1950s–1970s." *American Political Science Review* 73:781–94.

Sunstein, C. 2001. *Republic.com*. Princeton: Princeton University Press.

Tate, Katherine. 1993. *From Protest to Politics: The New Black Voters in American Elections*. New York: Russell Sage Foundation.

Tidmarch, Charles M., Lisa J. Hyman, Jill E. Sorkin. 1984. "Press Issue Agendas in the 1982 Congressional and Gubernatorial Election Campaigns." *The Journal of Politics* 46:1226–42.

Truman, David B. 1971. *The Governmental Process*. New York: Knopf.

Valentino, Nicholas A., Vincent L. Hutchings, and Ismail K. White. 2002. "Cues That Matter: How Political Ads Prime Racial Attitudes during Campaigns." *American Political Science Review* 96(1): 75–90.

Verba, Sidney, Nancy Burns, and Kay Lehman Schlozman. 1997. "Knowing and Caring about Politics: Gender and Political Engagement." *Journal of Politics* 59:1051–72.

Verba, Sidney, and Norman H. Nie. 1972. *Participation in America.* Chicago: University of Chicago Press.

Verba, Sidney, Kay Lehman Schlozman, and Henry E. Brady. 1995. *Voice and Equality: Civic Voluntarism in American Politics.* Cambridge: Harvard University Press.

West, Darrell M. 1994. "Political Advertising and News Coverage in the 1992 California U.S. Senate Campaigns." *Journal of Politics* 56:1053–75.

Whitby, Kenny J., and Franklin D. Gilliam, Jr. 1991. "A Longitudinal Analysis of Competing Explanations for the Transformation of Southern Congressional Politics" *Journal of Politics.* 53:504–18.

Wolfinger, Raymond, and Steven J. Rosenstone. 1980. *Who Votes?* New Haven: Yale University Press.

Wolpert, Robin M., and James G. Gimpel. 1997. "Information, Recall, and Accountability: The Electorate's Response to the Clarence Thomas Nomination." *Legislative Studies Quarterly* 22:535–50.

Wright, Gerald C., and Michael B. Berkman. 1986. "Candidates and Policy in the United States Senate Elections." *American Political Science Review* 80:565–88.

Yeric, Jerry L., and John R. Todd. 1996. *Public Opinion: The Visible Politics.* 3d ed. Itasca, IL: Peabody Publishers.

Zaller, John R. 1992. *The Nature and Origins of Mass Opinion.* New York: Cambridge University Press.

———. 1996. "The Myth of Massive Media Impact Revived: New Support for a Discredited Idea." In *Political Persuasion and Attitude Change,* ed. Diana C. Mutz, Paul M. Sniderman, and Richard A. Brody. Ann Arbor: University of Michigan Press.

Index

Page references in italics indicate an illustration; page references followed by *t* indicate a table.